LEGENDS
of
THE RHINE

"O, the pride of the German heart is this noble river!

And right it is; for of all the rivers of this beautiful earth

there is none so beautiful as this."

— W. W. Longfellow

selected and edited
by
Joanne Asala

Penfield
Press

About the Editor

Joanne Asala majored in medieval literature at the University of Iowa. She is the author of numerous titles including *German Proverbs, Proverbs of the North: Words of Wisdom from the Vikings, Swedish Proverbs and Norwegian Proverbs.*

Acknowledgements

Editors: Dr. Eberhard Reichmann, Joan Liffring-Zug Bourret, Dorothy Crum and Melinda Bradnan.

Cover design by Molly Cook, assisted by Mary Martin, M.A. Cook Design.

Illustrations are from the collection of Dr. Eberhard Reichmann and others, including *Das Blaue Buch vom Rhein,* Karl Robert Langewiesche Nachfolger, Hans Köster, Königstein, Taunus; *Heath's Picturesque Annual,* 1833, from drawings by Clarkson Stanfield, Esq.; and map drawings by Hans Otto Buchner, Partenkirchen.

Books by Mail
(postpaid prices subject to change)

Legends of the Rhine (this book) $16.95
Germany's Regional Recipes: Foods, Festivals, Folklore $18.95
German Proverbs $14.95
German-American Life: Recipes and Traditions $16.95
Great German Recipes $6.95
German Recipes: Old World Amana $13.95

Send $2.50 for a complete catalog of all German-related and other titles available.
Please send orders to Penfield Press, 215 Brown Street, Iowa City, Iowa 52245

Contents

Preface

In 1438, ecstatically praising the Rhine, the Italian traveler Enea Silvia Piccolomini noted, "…nowhere in Europe is a river so adorned with so many significant cities; although surpassed in length by many, none are surrounded by greater nobility and charm…" This is but one of numerous tributes paid by visitors overwhelmed by the Rhine regions' natural and man-made beauty.

Originating in Switzerland, passing a stretch along the French border, and eventually leaving Germany for Holland and its destination in the North Sea, the Rhine is not only the most traveled international waterway, it is the river that runs right through the German soul. It has been celebrated in song and dance, in poetry and prose and art, ever since the days of Roman settlement on its banks and vicinity more than 2,000 years ago. Especially on the Middle Rhine, where it has carved its path through several mountain ranges, there are more romantic castles and castle ruins, often surrounded by steep vineyards, than anywhere in the world.

Local legends are populated with both noble and evil knights and princes, bishops and priests, rich and poor, giants and dwarfs, beautiful women and fairies. And, as in real life, goodness and wickedness alternate as these characters pass in review. The legends' short prose depicts strange and phantasmic events, often embracing the supranatural. But unlike the fairy tale, located in never-never land and "once upon" an indefinite time, legends are typically attached to specific places or regions and periods. As they were retold through the generations and as they spread beyond their places of origin they were modified and adapted to changing tastes.

Not until the early nineteenth century did this rich oral legend tradition catch the attention of collectors and researchers. The Brothers Grimm, Jacob and Wilhelm, famous for the fairy tales they passed on to posterity, were also the driving force for the preservation of the legends. Joanne Asala's present English-language edition of selected *Rheinsagen* opens a treasure chest of worthwhile reading for a new generation of readers.

— Eberhard Reichmann, Ph.D.
Max Kade German-American Center
Indianapolis, Indiana

The Rhine Song

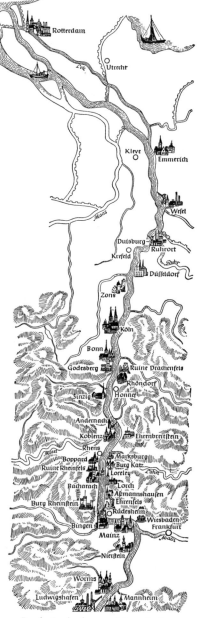

The Rhine! That little word will be
For aye a spell of power to me
And conjure up, in care's despite,
A thousand visions of delight:
The Rhine! Oh, where beneath the sun
Doth our fair river's rival run?
Where dawns the day upon a stream
Can in such changeful beauty shine
Outstripping Fancy's wildest dream,
Like our green, glancing, glorious Rhine.

Born where the blooms of Alpine rose,
Cradled in the Bodensee,
Forth the infant river flows,
Leaping on in childish glee.
Coming to a riper age,
He crowns his rocky cup with wine,
And makes a gallant pilgrimage
To many a ruined tower and shrine.
Strong, and swift, and wild, and brave,
On he speeds with crested wave:
And spurning aught like check or stay,
Fights and foams along his way
O'er crag and shoal until his flood
Boils like manhood's hasty blood.

—From *Legends and Lays of the Rhine*

*Ludwigshafen – Mannheim
to the North Sea*

6

Stavoren
The Sunken City

Where the waves of the Zuyder Zee now roll, there was once, according to tradition, a blooming and prosperous tract of land. And on the very spot where fishermen now anchor their boats to cast their nets, there rose a beautiful city, carefully protected from the ever-encroaching sea by massive dikes. The inhabitants of Stavoren, for such was the name of this town, were very wealthy indeed. They had so much money, in fact, that they paved their banqueting halls with shining gold ducats. But, in spite of their prosperity, they were selfish, hardhearted and neglectful of the poor.

The wealthiest among them was a maiden named Rychberta. She had counting houses, farms, palaces and fleets, but her only thought, night and day, was how she might gather more.

One bright autumn morning she summoned the captain of the largest vessel in her fleet and said to him, "You have a year and a day to return with a cargo of the most precious and best of all earthly substances. Do not dare to return until you have done so."

The captain shook his head and laughed, "Surely you must have an object in mind? How am I to find something when I don't know whether or not it exists?"

"Such insolence!" Rychberta spat. "I have told you all you need to know. The rest is up to you. Now go! Your presence is beginning to annoy me."

Forced to set sail at a venture, the captain left Stavoren. As soon as they were out of sight of the city, the captain called together his officers and crew. "Gentlemen, I am at a loss," he sighed. "I do not know what it is our lady desires, and so do not know in which direction to steer our course. What is the most precious and best of all earthly substances?"

7

Homeward Bound

Each man, of course, had his own opinion of what the most precious substance could be, and no two opinions were alike. "Gold!" cried some. "Diamonds!" cried others. "Spices!" cried a third group.

But none of these seemed right. "Our lady has more than enough gold and jewels, and her spice cabinets are full to overflowing. What more could she possibly ask?"

After much reflection, and the smoking of many a pipe, a young crewman suddenly cried, "My captain, I have it!"

"Yes, yes? What is it, boy?"

"Sir, what could be more precious than wheat, the staff of life?"

"Of course!" the captain's face broke into a wide grin. Pleased with the resourcefulness of his crew, he immediately set a course for the Baltic to purchase a cargo of the finest grain. Proudly he sailed back to the port of Stavoren, arriving long before the year was ended. "Won't my lady be pleased!" he thought to himself.

Rychberta, in the meanwhile, had told all of Stavoren that her vessel had gone in search of a cargo of the best and most precious of all earthly things. No amount of coaxing from friends or relations could get her to reveal what the cargo might be. "You'll just have to wait and see!" she smugly replied.

But when her captain suddenly appeared before her, and informed her that he had brought a cargo of wheat, her complacency vanished. She flew into a terrible rage, and screamed, "You idiot! You dolt! What a fool you have made of me. All of Stavoren must be laughing up their sleeves. I want every kernel—every kernel—of that infernal grain immediately cast into the sea!"

"My Lady!" the captain begged. "If you do not want the wheat, shouldn't it be given to the poor?"

"Dump it all in the sea," she repeated. "I will come down to the port in person to make sure it is done. Now leave my sight!"

Sadly retracing his steps to the vessel, the captain met several hungry beggars. "There is nothing I can do for you," he told them. "My lady Rychberta has demanded that the wheat be thrown away."

First shock and then despair swept through the crowds. By the time Rychberta reached the dock, the poor had assembled from all parts of the city in hopes of securing a bowl of the unwanted grain. In spite of their pleas, however, the haughty lady made the sailors cast all the wheat into the sea while the captain, powerless to stop this sinful waste, looked on in rage. As the last kernel vanished beneath the waters, he turned to his mistress and through clenched teeth spoke. "That grain would have fed the poor for many months. Perhaps the entire winter! As surely as there is a God above us, you will be punished for this cruelty. As I live and breathe, I hope to see a time when you, the wealthiest woman in Stavoren, will long for a few handfuls of this squandered wheat. I can no longer work for such a horrible creature!"

The lady listened to these words in angry silence. Slowly she drew from her slim white hand a gold and diamond ring. She held it high for all the crowd to see, and then threw it into the crashing waves. "When next I see that ring, perhaps I will credit your words," she sniffed. And as she turned away she glanced over her shoulder, "As if anyone could believe a day would come when I should face such want."

That self-same evening, in preparing a fresh fish for dinner, Rychberta's cook found the costly ring resting in the sea creature's stomach. She immediately had a kitchen aide bring it to their proud mistress, too fearful to do the task herself. The lady grew very pale when she recognized the jewel, and fought for words to say. At that moment a messenger came rushing in to report, in quick succession, the ruin of her counting houses, the destruction of her fleet, the burning of her palaces, and the devastation of her farms. In the course of a few hours, she found herself shorn of all her wealth, for even her house burned down to the ground during the night. She was lucky to escape with her life.

Now that her money was gone, the wealthy of Stavoren refused to recognize Rychberta and the poor, who had met with nothing but contempt and mistreatment at her hands, allowed her to die of hunger and cold on the streets.

This sudden downfall, and the punishment of the proud lady, did not produce any effect at all upon the other rich people of Stavoren. They continued to enjoy life as before, and to neglect their fellow creatures. So a second warning was sent to them. Little by little they heard that the port was becoming unmaneuverable. Far down in the bed of the sea the squandered grains of wheat germinated, and a harvest of bare stalks grew until it reached the surface of the water. The shifting sands at the bottom of the sea were bound together by the overspreading stalks into a mighty sandbar, which soon rose above the waves, hindering all further commerce. The people, gazing upon it, called it "The Lady's Strand" in mocking honor of Rychberta.

No longer were merchant vessels able to enter the harbor. Many a ship was dashed to pieces by the fury of the breakers, and Stavoren become a ghost port. While the rich cared but little for the closing of their port, the poor suffered more sorely still, for now they were even deprived of the small pay they had received for their work of loading and unloading vessels.

This second warning also fell upon deaf ears, yet Providence granted the rich another reprieve, and gave them a third and final warning. A little leak was discovered in the dike through which the sea, filtering into the city reservoir, rendered the city waters undrinkable. Laughingly the rich vowed, "If we cannot drink water, let us then drink champagne." But when the thirsty poor crowded around their gates, imploring a sup of beer, they rudely dismissed them, the cruelest of them declaring, "If you think you shall die of thirst, perhaps you should hurry up and get it over with."

That selfsame night, when the last reveler had sunk into a deep sleep, the sea finished the work of destruction, breaking down the dikes and, bursting over Stavoren, submerging the whole town.

Over the spot where the proud city once stood, the waves now ripple in the sunlight, or are thrashed into foam by the cold wind sweeping down from the north. Boatmen, rowing out from the dilapidated little fishing town, which alone now bears the name of the ancient city, sometimes rest upon their oars, when the waters are smooth and clear, to point out far beneath them the palaces, turrets, and ramparts of Stavoren.

Father Rhine, *by Moritz von Schwind (1848)*

The Hague
The Beggar's Curse

Countess Kristiana, a wise and thrifty woman, was busy each day from sunrise until sunset. Thanks to her hard work and penny-pinching ways, her home was the finest, her cattle the fattest, and her servants the best dressed of all the people in Henneberg.

After issuing orders to her farmhands and stable boys, conferring with the cook over the day's menu, and carefully inspecting her household, she always retired to the great hall where all her maids sat spinning. It was here, while watching and directing their labors, that she kept her own wheel humming ceaselessly.

One morning the aged porter entered the spinning room. "Mistress?" he called, twisting his apron nervously between his hands. "There's a wo…"

"What is it Jan?" exclaimed the countess in displeasure. "Aren't you supposed to be polishing the brass on the front door?"

"Th-there's a woman here to see you ma'am. Sh-she says that it is urgent."

"Not another one, Jan!" the countess sighed. "How many times must I tell you that I will not encourage begging? Why doesn't this woman work? Does she expect to eat her bread in idleness?"

"Do you want me to send her away?"

"No," she snapped as she rose from her seat and checked her whirling wheel. "I see I must put an end to this myself. I shall personally dismiss her!" Giving a sharp glance to her maids she added, "Do not think my absence allows you an early rest, my dears. Idle hands are the devil's." The Countess Kristiana left the room and hurried along the echoing hall to the great door, where the poor woman anxiously awaited her.

"Please, your Ladyship," said the woman in a voice most piteous. "I have nothing to eat, and my children are so hungry."

"Nothing to eat!" repeated the countess, glancing contemptuously at the poor woman standing before her with a bundle in each arm. "You must work, my good woman. Only those who earn their bread by the sweat of their brow have any right to eat."

"But, noble Lady, I cannot work. The children are so small they need all my care," cried the poor woman. She parted the threadbare rags to show the pale, pinched faces of two tiny, newborn babes. "And last week, only last week, gracious Lady, my poor husband was drowned in the Rhine!"

"What?" cried the countess. "Two children? Twins?! What business have you, a beggar, to have any children at all?"

"Gracious Lady!" cried the poor woman. "The Lord sent me these children, and now I cannot bear to hear them cry. Help me, Lady, help me!"

"My good woman," said the countess reprovingly, "the Lord surely had nothing to do with those children. Do you suppose He would send two children at once to a poor woman like you, who has not the means to feed even one? I could feed scores, yet I have no children. No, no, the Lord has more sense. The Evil One must have sent you those."

"The Evil One, Lady!" cried the indignant mother, clasping her babies closer still. "It was the Lord sent them, and I curse you for your evil suggestion. I pray that our dear Lord bless you with as many children as there are days in the year. Then, my Lady, when you hear them cry you will perhaps understand what a mother feels."

With tears streaming down her pale face, the woman turned and left the castle. The countess, feeling she had wasted too many precious moments listening to such nonsense, hastened back to her wheel. At the sound of her step, and the jingle of the keys she always wore at her girdle, the merry maids immediately stopped their innocent chatter. When the countess entered the room, the shining heads were diligently bending over their tasks. Naught could be heard but the hum of the wheels.

Kristiana resumed her own chores. But no matter how fast the countess drove her wheel, it only seemed to echo the beggar-woman's curse: "May the Lord send you as many children as there are days in the year." Day after day, week after week, month after month, the prophecy haunted her, and her servants shook their heads as she daily became more harsh and exacting.

But a day came at last when all the spinning wheels in the great hall stood motionless, when the stools before them remained unoccupied, and when, instead of a busy hum, wailing cries echoed throughout the castle. In answer to the beggar woman's prayer, the good Lord had sent three hundred and sixty-five infants to the hardhearted countess. In vain the noble lady wept and wrung her hands as one by one she birthed the children. The babes were hers, as witnessed by the troop of mid-wives, and she could not disown them.

Terrified of the new duties imposed upon her, driven almost frantic by the children's cries, and appalled at the thought of the havoc which so many busy hands and feet would make in her orderly household, the noble Countess of Henneberg fell back upon her pillows and breathed her last.

But the children survived. All 365 infants were strong and healthy. The Count of Henneberg, proud as any father could be, decreed they should all be carried to the church and duly bap-tized. "Whatever shall you name them?" asked the priest. "There are so many!" After much thought, the count decided that com-ing up with individual names would have been too great a task, and so he decided that all the boys should bear the name of Johann, and all the girls that of Elisabetha.

This christening, the largest on record, was performed whole-sale, and the basin used for the ceremony has ever since been exhibited as a curiosity in one of the principal churches of the Hague. You may see it for yourself.

Cleves
The Prince's Vow

O tto, the youngest son of the noble family of Hesse, was destined from his cradle to enter a monastery. For centuries each generation had yielded a son to the contemplative life, and Otto was honor bound to fulfill his duty. Yet the handsome and wild young man shuddered in horror at the thought of a life without music, dancing, and women. No matter how much he wished to please his father, and how hard he worked at his studies, poor Otto could not resign himself to meet his fate.

Alone and in the dead of night, he escaped from home disguised as a mercenary, and bravely set out to seek his fortune. Several days' journey brought him at last to the city of Cleves, where his great skill with the crossbow soon won the duke's favor.

Knights and ladies of high degree crowded around him, applauding his handsome figure and unerring aim. But no praise seemed to gratify him half as much as the radiant smile with which the duke's lovely daughter hailed each successful shot. Hour after hour and day after day Otto most diligently practiced with his longbow beneath the maiden's window. The duke's daughter would often reward the young man with a shy smile and a wave. Obviously Cupid, the famous archer of lore, had shot his own arrows into the hearts of these two young lovers.

One day, when Otto could again be found beneath his love's window, the arrival of a familiar knight caused him for a moment to stay his hand. A chill of dread went down his spine. Instead of pausing to answer the duke's welcome, this stranger suddenly rushed forward and fell at Otto's feet with the joyful cry, "My Lord and Master, I have found you at last!"

"I-I-I don't know what you're talking about," replied Otto shakily.

"Your father has sent me to find you. You are to be brought home immediately to fulfill your sacred duty."

"What is this?" the duke interrupted. "Are you to say that my new archer is a nobleman?"

But before the messenger could answer, Otto called up to the maiden's tower, "Farewell, my love. I will find a way for us to be together!" He then darted through the open gate with the speed of one of his own arrows and vanished into the neighboring forest.

Slowly the errant knight rose to his feet, gazed after the fleet-footed youth with a look of despair, and only then turned to answer the duke. "That was my lord Otto, youngest son of the noble family of Hesse. He was to honor the family by dedicating himself to a life of contemplation, but all that has changed. His elder brothers have all died without leaving issue. Otto doesn't know. I was to bring him back to the castle. Only now…"

"Hmmm…" said the duke. "Why don't you come inside, my good Sir. We were just about to sit down to a feast. We can discuss this problem, you and I. Otto is a remarkably good archer, but I think I can force him to acknowledge I am a better marksman than he."

While slowly sipping his Rhine wine before a blazing fire, the duke proposed a plan for the recovery of the fugitive prince. At the duke's call, archers, knights, and men-at-arms crowded into the hall. There they received orders to sally forth and not return until they had captured the missing youth. "But, I solemnly charge you not to injure a hair of his handsome young head," continued the duke as he gave them the signal to depart.

With a loud cheer, the host rushed out the castle gates and began to surround and beat the forest. The duke turned to the messenger and slyly exclaimed, "Now, Sir Knight, I'll bait the trap."

With a nod and smile of approval, Otto's servant watched the duke enter his daughter's apartment. When the duke returned at the end of half an hour, gleefully rubbing his hand, the messenger anxiously inquired, "Well, most noble Duke, is it all settled? Did you experience any difficulty in winning your daughter's consent and connivance?"

"None whatsoever," answered the duke, laughing so heartily that the armor hanging around the great hall fairly rang. "The altar is dressed, the candles lit, the priests ready, and unless I am very much mistaken, my men are even now bringing the victim…er…bridegroom."

The words were scarcely out of his mouth when archers and horsemen burst into the hall dragging Otto, whose torn garments, disheveled locks, and exhausted appearance fully corroborated their statement that he had led them a lively chase.

"Take him into the church immediately," commanded the duke in his sternest tones. "I will not allow disobedience. Drag him to the altar, where he will have to take his vows."

"Never!" exclaimed Otto passionately. "Never! You may drag me into the church and to the altar steps, but not one word will pass my lips. I'd rather die than take a single vow!"

"We will see, fair Sir; we will see," said the duke. Paying no further heed to the young man's protests, he led the way to the church.

But when they had entered the sacred edifice, and Otto beheld a familiar, graceful figure all clad in white and enveloped from head to foot in a snowy veil, he suddenly ceased to offer any resistance. Like a man in a dream, he was led up the aisle and, obeying the duke's imperative sign, knelt beside the vision.

Instead of the dreaded consecration service, the priests now began the marriage ceremony. Otto suddenly forgot his rash declaration, and with a firm and eager voice gladly took the vows which were to bind him forever, not to the church, but to a beloved and blushing bride.

The service concluded, the Duke of Cleves stepped forward to offer his congratulations, explaining to Otto the change which had taken place in his fortunes.

"And now, Landgrave of Hesse, my noble son-in-law, unless you sorely repent taking your vows at the altar a few moments ago, in spite of your loudly declared determination to die rather than do so, it behooves you publicly to confess that I am a better archer than you, for I have hit the mark!" exclaimed the duke merrily.

"You may be the better marksman, Sir Duke!" exclaimed Otto, as he rapturously clasped his bride to his heart. "But you cannot deny that I have secured the prize!"

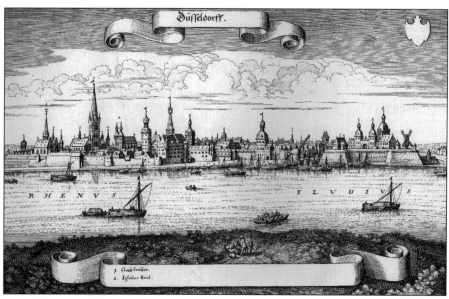

Düsseldorf, Westphalia, *by Matthäus Merian (1647)*

Liège
Saint Peter and Saint George

Saint Peter, weary of opening and shutting the Gates of Heaven and longing to visit the fair spot on earth which bears the name of Liège, once summoned Saint George and entreated him to take his place for a little while.

Good Saint George, ever ready to oblige, cheerfully acquiesced. He studied the fastenings and opened and shut the gates until he felt sure he thoroughly understood their mechanism. Then he solemnly promised his colleague to refuse admittance to none who knocked, and to patiently answer their every question.

Saint Peter was about to depart when Saint George suddenly detained him by exclaiming: "Hold, Peter! I don't know one word of French! Suppose a Frenchman should knock at the gate!"

"No danger!" replied Saint Peter reassuringly. "No danger, my good fellow. Many a century has come and gone since I first took charge of the Heavenly Gates, but although persons of almost every nation have presented themselves, no Frenchman has ever yet appeared to seek admittance."

Then Saint Peter departed, and for a while Saint George undertook the office of porter. Although he was called upon to answer countless questions and admit many souls, the Germans aver he had no occasion to do violence to his tongue, for no Frenchman knocked at the Gates of Heaven.

Cologne
The Architect of Cologne

E ngelbert the Holy, Bishop of Cologne, longed to signalize his rule and immortalize his name by some great work. He determined, therefore, to erect a cathedral which would tower far above and outshine all others. With this laudable purpose in view, he sent for a renowned architect.

"Thank you, your Honor!" cried the architect. "I hope I can fulfill all your expectations."

"You had better," cautioned the bishop, "or else your reputation will be worth naught. I want this cathedral to be the finest ever seen in the Rhine Valley, and quite unlike any other cathedral in existence."

The architect was delighted with the honor imposed upon him. He returned to his own humble little dwelling, spread a huge sheet of spotless parchment upon the table before him, and prepared his rules, compasses, and other drawing implements. "Aha," he said, and then, "aha" again. But the smooth, clean parchment stared back at him mockingly. Inspiration entirely failed him.

Hour after hour the architect pondered, but the great sheet still remained a perfect blank. "Perhaps if I take a walk to clear my head..." he mused. He wandered along the crooked, narrow streets of Cologne and down to the banks of the Rhine. A stretch of fine, smooth sand invited him to take pause. Idly, at first, he began tracing the outline of a cathedral in the sand; then suddenly he grasped his cane more firmly and drew more rapidly, until, in his excitement, his breath came in quick, short gasps. Dome, turrets, and spire were added one by one, and when all was finished, he raised his head and proudly shouted to the heavens, "There is the cathedral plan! Surely none can ever equal it."

"No. None but the cathedral of Mayence, of which that is a very fair copy," said a mocking voice close beside him.

The architect, who until then had believed himself quite alone, now turned with a start and beheld a wizened little old man bent over his plan. A sarcastic grin spread over his sharp face. The architect's first impulse was, of course, to strike the odd little man in anger, but with a second glance at the cathedral in the sand he knew the criticism was true.

Hastily the architect rubbed out the outline, smoothed the sand, and patiently began to trace a second plan. Under his practiced hand, choir, nave, altar and chapel rapidly assumed beautiful and harmonious proportions. Like one inspired, he added ornament and tracery, carefully elaborating his design. When the last touch had been given, he stood off a few paces and triumphantly cried, "There! Such an edifice as that has never yet pierced the blue vault of heaven!"

"No. None save the cathedral of Strassburg," snickered the same derisive voice.

Again the architect's hopes were dashed to the ground. "Strassburg!" he exclaimed. "Strassburg! Arrggh...yes! It's true, all too true!" His head sank down upon his breast and the light of pleasure died out of his eyes. But he was a determined man, and a moment later he gathered his strength and began a third plan, muttering that he would surely have time to complete it before the sun set and darkness overtook him.

His hand fairly trembled with eagerness and his eyes almost started from their sockets as he tried to represent the visions of beauty which now thronged his brain. The cane moved faster and faster, the lines covered the sand like network; the red disk of the sun sank beneath the distant horizon, and its rosy glow was reflected in the sparkling Rhine as the last line was rapidly traced.

"There!" he cried. "This is no treacherous effect of memory, but a creation of my own brain which will make my name immortal!"

"Ha! Ha! Ha!" chuckled the little old man. Once again the architect had entirely forgotten his presence. "You are mistaken,

Sir Architect. What you so proudly call a creation of your own brain looks singularly like the cathedral of Amiens."

The architect could not but acknowledge the similarity. Beside himself with anger and completely baffled, he threw his staff at the stranger's feet and impetuously cried, "Perhaps you could draw a better plan!"

The clawlike fingers immediately closed over the staff and in the rapidly gathering twilight the stranger traced the plan, cut, and elevation of a stupendous cathedral. With dilated eyes the architect breathlessly followed his every movement, and although the lines were so quickly and faintly traced that they were lost to sight almost as soon as made, he still saw enough to be convinced that the plan far surpassed anything that he had yet seen.

"Well, what do you think of my plan?" asked the old man.

"It is simply stupendous!" sputtered the architect. "But who are you, who can thus, in a very few moments, create such an exquisite plan? You are surely the greatest architect on the face of the earth, or…"

"His Satanic Majesty, the greatest architect in the Lower World, at your services, Sir Architect. Moreover, if my plan pleases you, it is yours. You shall reap all the honors and profits which it cannot fail to bring you, if you will only consent to pledge me your soul in exchange."

"May the Holy Mother protect me!" cried the terrified architect, vehemently crossing himself again and again. With a snarling cry of rage the fiend vanished and the architect found himself alone, by the rushing river, once more. No trace of his companion remained except a lingering odor of brimstone. The cathedral plans were also gone—wiped away as if they had never existed.

With hasty, trembling steps, the architect returned home, and all night long he tossed about, sleepless, on his couch, vainly striving to recollect the plan of the cathedral which hovered vaguely and tantalizingly before him. But, in spite of all his efforts, he could not reproduce even the most simple detail.

Day after day passed. The appointed meeting with the bishop was almost upon him, and still, the architect was no nearer his goal than at first. Once more he wandered to the banks of the swift-flowing Rhine and there, in the gathering twilight, the fiend once more appeared before him.

"The plan is still at your disposal, Sir Architect," he murmured in soft, conspiratorial tones. "Subscribe to my conditions, and you shall have it."

As in a dream, the architect beheld the finished cathedral and heard the cries of an enthusiastic multitude praising his name. Overcome by the temptation, he quickly gasped, "I consent! The plan, give it to me, quick!"

"Meet me here tomorrow at midnight," answered the tempter. "As soon as you have signed your name to a certain little pledge, which I shall have the honor of laying before you, the plan will be yours."

The thought of submitting such an exquisite plan to Engelbert the Holy, and the glory, which would ever rest like a halo upon his name, danced in the architect's mind. But when night closed in and he found himself all alone in his room, the recollection that his soul would be lost forever came upon him with all its force. With loud groans and many tears, he sank upon his knees to entreat aid from Heaven. But when he would have prayed, he could find no suitable words, and could only repeat, over and over again, the short conversation which had taken place between him and the fiend.

His housekeeper, awakened by his groans, grew pale with horror as she crouched by the keyhole and heard every word. Tremblingly, she put on her hooded cloak, stole out of the house door and hobbled off to church, where she poured out the whole story into the astonished ears of her father-confessor. "Please, Father, you must save him. He is really a good man, kind and considerate."

The priest, who had listened very attentively, pondered the matter for a while and then began to explain to the tearful, anxious woman that a plan sufficiently beautiful to induce her master to pledge his soul for its possession must be obtained at almost any price. "What is one man's soul against such a glory to God? People will flock to Cologne to see our wonder."

"What!?" cried the housekeeper. "You cannot possibly mean that."

"Well," sighed the priest. "I suppose we should make every effort to rescue a human soul, if it is possible." Producing a piece of the true cross, set in gold and precious stones, he bade the housekeeper to give it to her master. "This is what you must tell him to do...."

The holy relic concealed beneath the dark folds of his mantle, the architect stole out alone, late at night, to keep his appointment with the devil. Not a star twinkled in the firmament above. The wind whistled and moaned as it blew over the river and touched his pale face with its clammy breath. Not a sound was heard in the city, save the dismal howls of a few dogs, until the bells slowly tolled the midnight hour. As the twelfth stroke died away, the Evil One suddenly appeared with a huge roll of parchment tucked under his arm.

"The plan! The plan!" gasped the architect, shivering with something besides the cold.

"It is here; you shall have it in a moment," answered Satan. "Just prick your finger with your penknife, use your blood to sign your name to this pledge, and the plan is yours."

The architect ransacked his pockets, but could not find his knife. Satan, who had anxiously watched his fruitless search, uttered an impatient groan and snapped, "Here, hold this plan for a moment while I look for a sharp stone."

For a moment the devil groped around in the darkness, but when he had found what he wanted and raised his head, he recoiled in horror. The architect stood before him, clasping the plan close to his breast and brandishing the relic of the true cross high above his head. Loudly he called, "Get thee behind me, Satan! Back, I say! In the name of the One who died upon this cross, I bid thee depart!"

Cowering in fear, his ugly features distorted by rage, Satan exclaimed, "Villain! You have outwitted me, but I shall yet have my revenge! The plan is yours—it is true—but the cathedral shall never be finished without my aid and consent. The story of your fraud will be noised abroad, but your name—instead of enduring forever—will soon be buried in oblivion!" With a threatening gesture Satan vanished.

The architect hastened home with the precious plan, which he had secured at such a terrible risk. Engelbert the Holy approved of it warmly, and the work was begun without delay. Countless workmen were employed, enormous sums were expended, and the architect, fondly hoping to outwit the Evil One a second time, had his name engraved in deep characters on one of the large stones of the tower. In his eagerness to see the effect, he sprang upon this block before it was properly secured, and as he leaned over, it tipped and fell to the ground, carrying him with it and crushing him to death beneath its weight.

Owing to this accident the work was stopped. Although often renewed, hundreds of years passed by ere the cathedral of Cologne was finally finished. It is, moreover, more commonly reported that it would still be incomplete had not Satan consented to its termination, and even contributed funds for the construction by establishing a famous lottery on its behalf. But, although the cathedral begun in 1225 was finished in 1880, the name of its real architect is still unknown.

Cologne
The Fire Bell

In one of the tall towers of Cologne Cathedral hung the Great Bell. Morning, noon and night it rang to call the faithful to prayers. Solemnly it tolled the flight of time, ever witnessing the passing months and years. Constant use gradually dulled its sound, however, and finally the city council declared that Wulf, the great founder, should fashion a new bell. Twenty-five thousand pounds of pure metal were purchased for its making.

Wulf made the mold, melted the metal, and invited all the people to witness the casting of the new cathedral bell. As he directed the streams of liquid metal into the mold, he proudly looked about him and, hoping to make a good impression upon the people, exclaimed, "God speed the casting!"

As he was an utter atheist, this prayer was not granted. When the mold was broken the bell was found useless. A wide crack ran from top to bottom. A second mold was prepared, a second casting made, and as the same mockery was again gone through with, the second bell also proved an utter failure.

Angry at this double mischance, Wulf prepared to make a third casting, and in his anxiousness exclaimed, "Devil take the work!" The people shuddered in horror at such impious words.

In spite of the founder's sin, the bell proved quite flawless. It was promptly hung in the tower, and Wulf was invited to be present so that his hand might ring the first melodious peal.

Pleased with the honor, the founder gave a mighty pull to the rope. "To the glory of God and my skill," he boasted. But instead of the harmonious sound he expected, the mighty bell gave forth a harsh, discordant tone as if all the fiends in hell were shrieking at once. The people anxiously crossed themselves and looked up at the tower with fear in their hearts. Wulf, shocked at the sound, started back in dismay and fell from the tower to his death.

The citizens left the great bell where it hung; not to summon the faithful to the house of God, but to warn the citizens of Cologne whenever some great danger was threatening them. Its harsh, grating tones are never heard, therefore, except in case of fire or war. When they rend the quiet air, the women and children cross themselves and pray, while the men gather forth to give the required aid.

Cologne with unfinished cathedral in the background upper right,
Heath's Picturesque Annual (1833)

Cologne
The *Heinzelmännchen*

Once upon a time, and a time before that, when the world was young and filled with magic, the inhabitants of Cologne were under the protection of the *Heinzelmännchen*. This tiny race of kind elves stole noiselessly into their homes at night and deftly finished all the work which had been set aside.

Each night the city's bakers would set their dough to rise, and when they awoke after a restful night's sleep they would find piles of newly baked loaves. The miller's grain was ground, and the flour tied up in sacks. The housewives rooms were swept and dusted. The spinner's flax was spun nightly, and the tailor in town always found the garments he had begun to cut out duly made and pressed, lying neatly folded upon his table.

Now the tailor's wife was a very inquisitive woman, and very anxious to see the mysterious *Heinzelmännchen*, who labored so kindly for them. As she was a heavy sleeper, she cast dry peas all over the floor before she went to bed one evening. The tiny *Heinzelmännchen*, racing to-and-fro in their busy haste, stepped on the peas, tripped and fell, making such a clatter with the irons, tongs, and scissors, that the tailor's wife, waking up, hastened to take a peep at them. "Hello! Hello!" she cried, night-cap askew and feet bare. "Welcome, welcome!"

The *Heinzelmännchen* guessed that it was this woman who had strewn peas on the floor, and they were quite indignant about it. "Nobody is to see us at our work!" they cried angrily. And without another word, they left the house and town forever. Since then, the people of Cologne have been obliged to do all their tasks unaided, and all the work which is not finished at nightfall is sure to be found in the same unsatisfactory state in the morning, for the *Heinzelmännchen* have vowed never to visit the town again.

Brauweiler
The Game of Chess

Otto III was but a child when his father died, leaving him heir to the Western Empire. Until he reached adulthood, the cares of government were entrusted to his mother and to a capable young nobleman named Ezzo, who had been one of the previous emperor's most trusted knights.

Young Otto was brought up at court under his mother's watchful eye, but his lovely sister, Princess Mathilda, was sent to the convent at Brauweiler. There she spent many years under the care of the nuns. The only time she ever left this quiet retreat was to witness the coronation of her brother, which took place as soon as he was of age to reign alone.

It was Count Ezzo's duty to retrieve the princess and accompany her to court. No sooner did he catch sight of the beautiful maiden than he fell deeply in love with her. His heart beat high with pleasure when he noticed that she seemed to prefer his society and conversation to that of all the other courtly knights.

His happiness was short-lived, however, for Mathilda soon returned to her convent home. Ezzo became so melancholy and absent-minded that the emperor began to marvel at the sudden change in his usually genial companion. "What is it, Ezzo?" he would ask. "Something is troubling you."

"It is nothing, my Lord," Ezzo insisted. "Do not worry yourself."

Thinking to divert the knight from this unknown sadness, Otto one day challenged Ezzo to a game of chess. "Let us make the game interesting!" he laughed. "Let the victor of three successive games ask the vanquished for any boon he desires. Whatever it is I shall grant you, and you in turn will give me what it is I most desire."

Pale and trembling with eagerness, for now his hopeless suit did not seem as hopeless, Ezzo began the game. He played so skillfully that he beat his sovereign all three times.

"You've beat me fairly," smiled the emperor. "What is it you desire?"

Falling at his monarch's feet, Ezzo asked in a trembling voice, "Would you be so generous as to offer me the hand of your sister, Mathilda, whose beauty and kindness shine above all other woman?"

Only momentarily taken aback, Otto agreed. "But you must seek her favor first. She may be my sister, but her destiny is her own."

Seeing the ill-suppressed anxiety and impatience of the suitor, Otto then laughingly bade him prepare to bear an important missive to the Brauweiler convent, telling him to be sure and wait until he received an answer to it in person. Ezzo, needless to state, was soon ready, and rode in haste to the convent, where, as bearer of an imperial message, he was allowed to see the Princess Mathilda alone.

The answer to the letter must have been all he could wish, for he soon informed the prioress that he had come to escort the princess to court, where she was to be married.

The prioress, hearing this news, shook her head in dismay, "Mathilda, the choice has been left in your hands. I urge you to select a heavenly rather than an earthly spouse."

"I'm not sure if it is me you will miss, or my dowry," said Mathilda. "But you are welcome to my marriage feast."

But the prioress shook her walking stick and angrily spat, "I'd soon believe this withered staff could again bud and bear leaves, than any good will accrue to you out of this alliance."

Ezzo, seeing the look of sadness cross over Mathilda's face at these words, suddenly caught the staff out of the Holy Mother's hand and thrust it deep into the earth near the convent door. "Let it remain there, Holy Mother," he growled. "We will see whether or not God approves of the union of loving hearts."

The marriage preparations were soon ended, the nuptial ceremony took place, and as the solemn benediction was pronounced over the newly married couple, the mulberry staff back at the convent put forth its first tiny little leaf. Little by little it grew and developed, until it became a mighty tree and flourished as proudly as Ezzo and Mathilda, who lived happily together, and whose many children grew up to be as good and happy as they.

The mulberry tree is still standing near the Brauweiler convent, at a short distance from Cologne. Whenever it shows any signs of decay, if true lovers kiss beneath its shade, it is sure to send forth a fresh shoot, which in due time replaces the withered and dried up tree.

St. Goar, *Heath's Picturesque Annual (1833)*

Arnoldsweiler
The Minstrel's Ride

A rnold the Minstrel once traveled with Charlemagne during a hunting expedition to the great Burgelwald forest. During the day he accompanied the emperor on his hunts, and in the evening he played courtly songs and ballads to the amusement of all in attendance. At noon, one day, the emperor bade Arnold sing to him and was so charmed with the minstrel's great talent that he promised to grant him as much land as he could ride around before the meal was ended. Arnold immediately sprang upon Charlemagne's own steed and rode rapidly away, scoring the tree-boles with his sword as he dashed by.

Even though the minstrel had urged the horse to its utmost speed, the animal had not gone very far before it began to show signs of fatigue. But Arnold, who had many friends in the woodlands, ruthlessly urged him on, only pausing to change steeds when he came upon a familiar homestead. Riding thus at full speed, and changing horses before their energy quite flagged, he rode around all the Burgelwald.

When he returned to the camp, the emperor laughingly remarked "You are evidently too modest, my good fellow. Our meal is not yet finished. How much land did you claim?"

"The whole forest!" exclaimed the minstrel, falling at the emperor's feet.

"What!" cried Charlemagne. "Of all the gall...."

"Forgive me, Sire, I only wish to secure the revenues of the Burgelwald for the benefits of the poor and sick," said Arnold humbly. "It was not for my own gain."

Charlemagne, touched by this humanity, gave him also the neighboring castle, which became the home of Arnold's descendants. They all cared for the poor as diligently as the minstrel, in whose honor the neighboring village of Arnoldsweiler is named.

Zundorf
The Crystal Palace

In the bed of the Rhine, between Zundorf and the little island of the same name, is the crystal palace of Father Rhine, if the report of a village midwife is to be believed. One night, when she was about to retire, this woman was suddenly called away from home by a taciturn man, enveloped in a great cloak and carrying a lantern that cast an eerie, phosphorescent glow.

Following him closely in the pouring rain, she stumbled along in the darkness until she felt cold water eddy around her ankles. She was about to jump back in terror when the man caught her in his arms and plunged with her right into the river. When she opened her eyes again, she found herself in a beautiful crystal palace, all set with precious stones, where she was shortly bidden to take good care of a beautiful golden-haired nymph named Undine.

The midwife was so efficient that before many hours had passed, her patient was comfortably settled and able to talk a little. In soft whispers, the golden-haired lady now confided to the old nurse that her husband was the mighty water spirit whom mortals called Father Rhine, while she was the only daughter of the Lord of Rheidt.

One day, clad in foamy green and disguised as a mortal, Father Rhine had appeared at the village dance and invited her to tread a measure with him. Whirling her around in ever widening circles, he had reached the river's edge and suddenly plunged with her into the stream. Ever since then, she had lived with him in the crystal palace as his most beloved of wives.

The fair young lady then cautioned the old woman to accept no more than the usual reward for her services, no matter how eagerly her husband might press her to accept rich gifts. She then closed her eyes in feigned sleep as Father Rhine appeared. Seeing his beloved wife entirely out of danger, the old river god beckoned to the nurse to follow him, and led her into his treasure chamber, where lay great heaps of gold, silver, and precious stones. "Help yourself!" he urged.

The old woman, mindful of the advice just received, passed by jewels and gold, and selected the small silver coins which were her usual guerdon. Resisting all her mysterious conductor's entreaties to take more, signified her readiness to depart. She knew well the cost of faerie gifts.

Taking her by the hand, Father Rhine then passed along a dark corridor, rose with her through the limpid flood, deposited her, dripping but safe on the shore near her native town, and vanished, after flinging a whole handful of gold in her lap. Ever since then, the simple people delight in telling of the marvels of the crystal palace beneath the flood. The old woman often described it minutely for the benefit of her admiring listeners, always producing a handful of gold in proof of the truth of her tale.

Rheinstein, *Heath's Picturesque Annual (1833)*

Godorf
The Will-o'-the-Wisp

The marshy peninsula which extends between Godorf and Rodenkirchen is said to be the favorite resort of the sprite known all along the Rhine as the Herwisch, and in England as the Will-o'-the-Wisp. This mischievous little creature is said to delight in leading unsuspecting travelers astray and in playing all manner of pranks. But, like most practical jokers, he is quick to resent any attempt to make fun of him.

One day a maiden, passing across this stretch of ground at nightfall, began to sing all the songs she knew to beguile the loneliness of the way and inspire her with courage. Having soon come to the end of her scanty repertoire, she carelessly sang a mocking ditty about the Herwisch who, enraged at her impudence, came rushing toward her threateningly brandishing his tiny lantern.

With a cry of terror, the girl began to run, closely pursued by the sprite who, in punishment for her derisive song, flapped his wings in her face and frightened her so badly that she became an idiot.

Since then, the young people of Germany have never dared to sing the mocking refrain, and carefully avoid mentioning the Herwisch's name after nightfall, lest they should in some way rouse his anger.

Bonn
The *Vehmegericht*

In the crypt of the cathedral of Bonn, which is said to have been founded by Constantine, were once held those famous midnight meetings of the German secret society called *Vehmegericht* which, in the Middle Ages, took the law into its own hands and executed summary justice. The *Vehmegericht* were as powerful and as feared as the Inquisition in Spain.

The Lord of Freyerwahl, a lawless robber knight, had long committed every sort of crime imaginable. Everyone had learned to fear and detest him. One day, while riding through a village, he caught a glimpse of a lovely young girl, a niece of the priest, whom he kidnapped that selfsame night. He even set fire to the parsonage to prevent immediate pursuit. The poor village priest lost all he had in the flames, but his deepest sorrow was caused by the total disappearance of his orphaned niece, of whom he could obtain no tidings.

One year after this calamity, which he had never ceased to mourn, the priest was summoned by an emissary of the *Vehmegericht*. In silence he was led into the crypt of the Bonn Cathedral at midnight. While waiting, the priest took note of the silent masked figures, the sable-hung walls, open grave, ax, block, rope and roll of parchment, which he knew were the emblems of the secret society.

All at once the silence was broken by the entrance of a prisoner who was accused of kidnapping a young lady and condemned to marry her. The Knight of Freyerwahl, for it was he, angrily refused to do so. In spite of all his struggles, the girl was brought in and, at an imperious sign from the judge, the priest performed the marriage ceremony.

As soon as the service was ended, and while the priest was rejoicing to see his niece once more, the judge went on to declare that the slight reparation just made to the poor girl's honor in no way balanced the crimes committed by the accused, who was then and there sentenced to death and executed. The guilty Lord of Freyerwahl's remains were duly interred in the cathedral, but the only inscription placed above them was his name, with the words: "Died by order of the Vehm, 1250."

Ehrenbreitstein, *Heath's Picturesque Annual (1833)*

Ramersdorf
The Cursed Dancers

Each Sunday afternoon, the inhabitants of the little hamlet of Ramersdorf assembled on the village green. Here the young people sang and danced merrily to the tune of flute and drum without a care that it was the Sabbath. Their elders would shake their heads and cross themselves, fearful of what was to become of their children.

As the year 1001 approached, matters changed. Many people believed in their hearts that the end of the world was at hand. The Sunday dances ceased, and the Abbot of Löwenberg saw his church crowded from morning till night with the somber faces of the village youths. Yet the much dreaded year came and passed without incident. The sun continued to rise and set; the seasons followed their course. Seeing no sign of coming ruin, the young people decided to resume their Sunday afternoon merrymaking. Scarcely had the fiddler raised his bow, however, when the abbot appeared among them. "Stop this sinful activity immediately," he demanded, "or face the wrath of heaven."

"Foolish old man," laughed their leader. "You warned us of the end of the world, too, and as you can see we're all still standing."

"You dare speak to me like that, a man of the cloth?" sputtered the abbot. "Then a curse on you all. If you so enjoy such pastimes, may you have to dance, unceasing, for a year and a day!"

A tremor of fear passed through the crowd as the words of the curse settled round them. The young people would have stopped their merry round, but to their dismay they found that they no longer had control over their feet. From that hour on they continued to dance until a year and a day had fully expired.

Night fell, and they ceased not; day dawned, and they danced still. In the heat of the noon, in the cool of the evening, day after day there was no rest for them. The seasons rolled over them. Summer gave place to autumn, winter succeeded summer, and spring decked the fields with early flowers as winter slowly disappeared. Yet still they danced on, through coursing time and changing seasons, with unabated strength and unimpaired energy. Rain nor hail, snow nor storm, sunshine nor shade seemed to affect them. Round and round and round they danced, in heat and cold, in damp and dry, in light and darkness. What were the seasons—what the times or the hour or the weather to them?

In vain did their neighbors and friends try to arrest them in their wild steps. In vain were attempts made to stop them in their whirling career. In vain did even the abbot himself interpose to relieve them from the curse he had laid on them, and to put a period to the punishment of which he had been the cause. No effort was left untried to relieve the dancers, but every one failed.

The sufferers themselves, however, appeared quite unconscious of what was passing. They seemed to be in a state of perfect peace, and to be altogether unaware of the presence of any persons, as well as insensible to pain or fatigue. But when the appointed end of their punishment arrived, they were all found huddled together in the deep cavity which their increasing gyrations had worn in the earth beneath them. It was a considerable time before sense and consciousness returned to them, and indeed, after, they never could be said to enjoy them completely for, although they lived long, they were little better than idiots during the remainder of their lives. Such was their curse.

Nonnen-Stromberg
The Hermit Sisters

In back of the little town of Königswinter on the Rhine, rise the seven hills known as the Siebengebirge, from whence beautiful views can be had of the Rhine and the surrounding country.

At one time, the Lord of Argenfels lived near these mountains. He had two beautiful daughters, Bertha and Mina, with whom he spent all his time. He was already well advanced in years and could no longer take any part in the military plans then afoot. All the country was in a great state of excitement at this time, for St. Bernard had been calling for a crusade, and his enthusiasm had inspired many knights to join the emperor Barbarossa against the Saracens.

This old Knight of Argenfels, although he could not take an active part in the campaign, nevertheless gave his money lavishly to further the cause. He warmly welcomed the knights who continually passed his gates on their way to the mustering at Frankfurt-am-Main.

One evening, he gave shelter to a handsome and brave young lord who dwelt on the Wolkenberg, one of the Seven Mountains. No sooner did the young man catch sight of the lovely Bertha than he entirely lost his heart to her. This knight made such good use of his short stay that when he rode away, it was as the betrothed of the fair maiden, who was to marry him as soon as he returned from the Holy Land.

Years passed and the Crusade, begun so hopefully, proved very disastrous, indeed. Many brave knights died in distant lands. The young Lord of Wolkenberg fell, like so many others, into the hands of the Saracens. For seven long years he was held prisoner. You can imagine how the poor lover pined for his sweet Bertha.

Each dawn found him in prayer. "I vow to build a chapel to St. Peter, if he will but let me out of this prison!" he wept.

At last his prayers were answered, and as soon as he was released, he hastened back to his native land. From afar he eagerly looked for the first glimpse of the lordly towers of Argenfels, and with a sharp pang saw that they were a mass of blackened ruins. Springing out of the boat at the landing, he hurried up the hill. An old shepherd told him that the castle had been besieged and taken by a robber knight. "The old Lord of Argenfels himself has fallen in the fray," the ancient peasant said, wiping a tear from his eye.

"And what of his daughters?" asked Lord Wolkenburg. "What news?"

"His daughters? Why, they must have perished also, for they have not been seen since."

The brokenhearted Lord of Wolkenburg withdrew to his lonely castle in the Siebengebirge, but, finding his sorrow unbearable, he resolved to consecrate the remainder of his life to God, and retire to some remote spot where he might erect a hermitage. He traveled far into the woods in search of a suitable place, and came at last to a little hut where, to his intense surprise and delight, he found his beloved Bertha and her sister.

After the first exchange of greetings had taken place, and the first rapture of meeting was over, the maiden told him how she and her sister had escaped, by an underground passage, from the besieged castle of Argenfels. They had taken refuge here, in the dense forest, to escape from the pursuit of their enemy. "He wished to marry me, to make his claim to our father's land legal and binding."

Needless to say, the Knight of Wolkenberg did not turn hermit, but married his lady love and built the chapel dedicated to St. Peter, which crowns the Nonnen-Stromberg, one of the Seven Mountains. It was here, too, that the other sister founded the convent in which she permanently took up her abode.

Nonnen-Stromberg
The Cruel Parents

On the Nonnen-Stromberg lived a cruel and unprincipled knight who, having lost all his sons, dragged his only daughter out of the convent of Villich, where she had already taken a nun's vows. "I will not have my line end here!" he growled. "You will marry and produce an heir."

In vain the poor young nun wept and protested. Her father declared she would be forced to obey, and to prevent her escape he kept her a close prisoner while he looked around for a suitable husband. A knight in the neighborhood, fully as wicked as he, finally suggested that his son should be the bridegroom. In spite of the young man's resistance, he commanded him to be ready on a certain day. "I will not hesitate to use force, should it become necessary," said his father.

The youth, who had lost his betrothed, had taken vows in the monastery of Heisterbach. His father did not care at all, and the poor son was dragged to the altar in rove and cowl to be joined by a tearful nun. Both stood motionless while a priest, bribed for the purpose, gave them the nuptial benediction. He had scarcely uttered the last words when the young couple, falling on their knees, fervently exclaimed, "In God alone we put our trust!"

With a terrible crash the ground opened under them and received their bodies, while their pure souls were seen by all the witnesses, soaring up into the open heavens, where hosts of angels met them with psalms of joy. The dishonest priest, terrified at this vision, rushed down the mountain which ever since then has been known as the Nonnen-Stromberg, the Nun's Mountain. His lifeless body was found in a ravine. As for the cruel fathers they lived unhappily, died miserably, and their souls—we can only guess—were claimed by Satan, whose faithful followers they had been all along.

Löwenberg
The Wild Hunt

The Löwenberg, another of the Seven Mountains, was once the daily hunting ground of a neighboring knight, who was so fond of the chase that he even hunted on Sundays. He once pursued his quarry to the foot of the altar where a priest was celebrating mass.

Outraged by the insolence of the knight, who then and there slew his game, the priest solemnly cursed him. At the same moment, the ground opened beneath the hunter's feet and a pack of hounds from the Infernal Region fell upon him and tore him to pieces.

Ever since then, on stormy nights, the knight's restless spirit hunts wildly through the air, followed by a spectral train of huntsmen and hellhounds, for he can find no rest, though dead, and is condemned to lead the Wild Hunt forever. Woe to the mortal who is caught out-of-doors when the hunt rides, for he may find himself their quarry.

Cologne, *Heath's Picturesque Annual (1833)*

Rheinbreitbach
The Three Miners

In the mountains near Rheinbreitbach are the oldest copper mines in Germany. Exhausted and filled with water, they are no longer a scene of such busy labor as they were a few centuries ago. No longer do the miners come from their homes in Rheinbreitbach to work all day in the dark passages underground. But the people of the village still talk of the "Three Miners" as though they lived only yesterday.

These miners, who were very good friends, always walked back and forth together from the village, and worked side-by-side, never failing to breathe a short prayer ere they went down into the shaft. But one morning, when there was a special pressure of work, they omitted the prayer, hurried down to their post, and were hard at work when they were startled by a long, ominous, rumbling sound and by the shaking of the ground around them. Simultaneously they rushed toward the shaft to escape, but they were too late. A huge mass of fallen earth and stones blocked the passage in which they found themselves. They were caught as surely as a mouse in a trap.

They called and shouted for help, although they knew it was impossible for any of their fellow workers to hear them. As their voices grew hoarse and ragged from the shouting, one of them turned to the others and said, "Let's save our strength, men. We need it to work our way out. There's food enough to last us a few days, and oil enough in our lamps for twelve hours."

"Agreed," said one of the others. "But let us now say the prayer we omitted this morning."

The three men lifted axes and began to dig their way out. But in spite of all their efforts, food, strength and light soon failed them. Clasping each other's hands they lay down in the darkness saying, "God's will be done."

They were resting quietly in the dark, sleep evading them, when a light suddenly appeared at one end of the gallery. Squinting against the sudden brightness, they beheld the approach of another miner. Yet this was not one of their fellow workers, but the Meister Hammerling, of whom they had heard many a tale. "It's a ghost, sure as we stand," breathed the leader of the trio.

"But I don't think he means any harm," whispered another. "I've heard he's a help to miners in trouble."

Drawing near them, the ghost addressed them in a voice as cold as the grave. "Here is a basket of food," he said to them. "While you remain beneath the earth, it shall never go empty. Here, too, is a lamp," he added, "so that you will always have enough light."

"Thank you," said the men. "But are you saying we shall live down here forever?" asked the leader.

"I am saying you must dig your own way out, and never forget the mercy of heaven. Whatever you wish for when you once again behold the sun's radiance shall be granted to you."

Meister Hammerling vanished without another word, but basket and lantern remained. The three miners, refreshed and encouraged, set to work again with renewed zest. Although their families in Rheinbreitbach mourned them as dead, they continued to dig their way out. For seven years, the lantern burned unceasingly, night and day, and the provision basket never ran out of food and drink. The three miners, having no way of counting time, little suspected how long they had been buried alive.

Finally the day came when a blow from their pickaxes let in the light of day. Then the lantern was extinguished; the basket was found empty. The three men returned hearty thanks to heaven for their rescue before they sought their homes in Rheinbreitbach.

Walking along briskly one exclaimed, "All I now wish is to clasp wife and children to my heart once more ere I die."

Speyer

"And I," replied the second, "shall be ready to leave the world forever when I have once more seen my family at table with me as usual."

"All I now ask," exclaimed the third, "is to linger for a year and a day with my loved ones, and then to be at rest."

A few minutes later the three miners entered the village where their appearance caused a great sensation, and where all crowded around them, scarcely able to believe the testimony of their own eyes.

As soon as the first miner had embraced his wife and children, he fell down dead. The second passed peacefully away after his first meal, and the third, having often recounted his adventures in the mine, slept to wake no more on earth at the end of a year and a day.

Landskrone and Neuenahr
The Wonder Bridge

Where the German river Ahr flows into the Rhine stand the ruins of the once lordly castle of Landskrone, directly opposite the fortress of Neuenahr. In the early Middle Ages the knights inhabiting these two castles were very good friends, indeed. In order to see each other daily, and as often as they pleased, they spanned the rushing stream with a high arched bridge, the marvel of the whole countryside, where it was known as the "Wonder Bridge." But these knights died, as all men do, and their successors quarreled and soon no one crossed the bridge.

A flock of birds, like none seen before, fell from the sky and filled the crevices between the stones of the bridge with a variety of seeds. These seeds sprouted and grew, covering the grey stones with an intricate tangle of flowering shrubs and creepers. Year after year passed by and the bridge, arching over the rushing waters with its burden of blossoms, was so picturesque that it deserved more than ever the title of the "Wonder Bridge."

Many centuries passed, and one of the castles became the property of a young knight. By accident, he met the young lady of the other castle at a tournament, and fell desperately in love with her. She felt the same, but unfortunately this damsel's father was not sympathetic. He rigidly kept up the family feud, although

47

the causes were long forgotten. The young people dared not openly proclaim their love.

They parted sadly when the festivities ended, and returned to their respective homes. While looking out of his window toward the abode of his beloved, the young knight's gaze suddenly fell upon the Wonder Bridge — so long unused — softly lit by the light of the moon. "Hmm," he mused, "the bridge once serviced the cause of true friendship. Perhaps it will equally serve love." Quietly he ventured out of the long-closed postern gate. Slowly, patiently, he worked his way through the flowery tangle, startling the sleepy birds and causing them to flutter away from their cozy nests.

The maiden, standing at her casement, saw the birds fly up into the evening sky. Holding her breath, hardly daring to dream it was true, she saw her lover draw near in the silvery moonlight. She hastened out to meet him, careful not to disturb her waiting women.

Night after night the lovers enjoyed their clandestine meeting, making plans for the future. "My father will never consent," the maiden sighed. "I don't know what we can do."

"I do," replied her lover confidently. "Follow me."

Gently and lovingly he helped her across the stream, and led her into the chapel of Landskrone where a waiting priest soon made them man and wife. The Wonder Bridge, having faithfully done its duty serving friends and lovers, gradually crumbled away into ruins, dropping stones into the water, one by one, until now no trace of it remains.

Dattenburg
The Ghostly Wedding

K urt von Stein was galloping wildly along the rocky road in a gorge not far from the Rhine, seeking a place where he might take shelter for the night. A storm was raging up the river valley and darkness was coming on rapidly. All at once he saw a light ahead of him, and coming nearer he saw the ruins of the ancient castle of Dattenburg. He roused the echoes by calling for a servant to come and take his horse. As no one answered his call, he soon dismounted and felt his way up the narrow winding stairs which led to the top of the tower where a light was shining brightly. When he came to the last step, he perceived an open door, and through it he saw a beautiful lady sitting by a table all alone.

In answer to his courteous request for shelter, the lady silently motioned him to enter. The table, bare a moment before, was soon covered with all manner of foods, of which she invited him by signs to partake. Somewhat awed by the maiden's beauty and silence, the knight obeyed, glancing about him from time to time and taking particular note of two portraits on the wall. He guessed these must represent the young lady's parents, as there was a great resemblance between them in spite of the antiquated garb.

After having finished his meal, Kurt von Stein ventured an interrogation, "Your parents, I suppose?" The maiden nodded. "Were they dressed for a costume party?" he politely inquired. "Their dress would seem to indicate that they had lived several centuries before."

To this the maiden only smiled, and von Stein concluded that the fair lady was mute. Continuing his conversation in the same vein, with her nodding or shaking her head in response, he soon discovered that she was an orphan and alone, the last of her family. Excited by her beauty, he began to woo her, and before many hours had passed, he was kneeling at her feet, entreating her to be his bride. Then, having won her consent, he saw her crown herself with a wreath of rosemary, and obeying her gesture, followed her down the stairs and into the castle chapel.

There he was surprised to see a numerous assembly of people in antiquated garb steal from behind pillar and tomb and silently take their places in the empty church. A moment later a bishop stepped down from the tomb on which he had been lying with folded hands, and marched gravely up to the altar to begin the service.

Kurt von Stein, sobered now and quailing with fear, vainly tried to speak the necessary answer to the priest's demand, whether he accepted that lady for wife, but, before he could recover the power of speech, the twelve solemn strokes from the convent of St. Helena reached his ear. "God have mercy upon me!" he suddenly exclaimed, and sank fainting to the ground.

When he recovered from his swoon, the sun was shining above him, the phantoms had disappeared, and he was alone in the ruined Dattenburg chapel. His steed grazed peacefully close beside him. Kurt von Stein hastened home, but as long as he lived, he vividly remembered the night he had spent in those ruins, and often gave thanks for having been saved from a marriage with the dead, for he felt that the lady could have been nothing but a ghost.

Rheineck
Desecrated Tombs

Having squandered most of his inheritance, Lord Ulrich of Rheineck was ever on the lookout to secure a new fortune, by any means—fair or foul.

One day, while this knight sat counting out his remaining gold coins, an old man knocked on the castle gates. Ulrich could no longer afford a porter, so he was forced to answer the door himself.

"Please sir," said the old man, "I am but a poor pilgrim on my way to Rome. Might I take shelter here this night?"

"Come in," urged Ulrich. "I haven't much to give you, only bread and a little water I carried up from the river myself. As you can see, I've fallen on hard times."

The pilgrim, amazed at this state of affairs, inquired, "Surely you must have some wine left in the cellar?"

"No," blushed the knight. "All the casks are dry."

"Perhaps you should look again," suggested the old man. "I will go with you."

Ulrich and the pilgrim were soon wandering through the great cellar where, in a remote corner, they finally found a well-concealed cask of rich old wine. "Ah," sighed the pilgrim after they drank down their first glass. "I've never tasted anything finer in all my journeys through the Rhine Valley."

A few more liberal glasses soon loosened Ulrich's tongue, and he told his guest of his own wish—to be wealthy once more.

"Hmm," the pilgrim mused, stroking his long whiskers. "If it's gold you desire, that can be satisfied easily enough. Not far from here there is an immense treasure, ready for the taking."

"You don't say!" exclaimed Ulrich. "Why haven't I heard of it?"

"The treasure is under the special protection of three witches.

But seeing as they are all on their way to their yearly Walpurgisnacht dance, you can easily enter the castle chapel at midnight and gain the riches for yourself."

"This castle?" Ulrich was incredulous.

"There's a treasure to be found beneath the bones of your family and ancestors. Break into their tombs and you will find gold aplenty."

Ulrich was, at first, greatly shocked by this proposal, but soon the greed for gold overcame all his scruples. The stroke of midnight found him in the ancient chapel. One by one he carried the moldering bodies of his ancestors outdoors and laid them on the grass. As he was bending over the last coffin, which contained the remains of a brother who had died in childhood, he was startled when the coffin lid was pushed aside and a tiny child sat up. "Brother, quick! Bring back the dead to their resting places before it is too late!" Without another word he crumbled into dry dust and bones.

Filled with nameless dread, Ulrich rushed out of the chapel to gather the earthly remains of his family. As he stepped through the doors he noticed that the pilgrim, whom he had left standing guard, had thrown off his disguise. It was none other than the Evil One himself. Clawlike fingers closed over the frightened man's arm as the beast growled in sinister tones, "Come, Ulrich, you are mine!"

But Ulrich cried, "In the name of Mary Mild, and of my poor helpless infant brother, I bid you to be gone!" The devil vanished at this command with a hoarse cry of rage.

The knight, miraculously saved from an awful fate, replaced his ancestors' bones in their tombs without pausing for a moment to search for the promised gold. On the morrow he began his own pilgrimage to Rome, humbly praying at every shrine by the way for the forgiveness of his sins.

Some years later, the villagers saw an aged pilgrim toil slowly up the hill of the abandoned castle. Failing to see him come down again, they went in search of him, and found him dead in the chapel. They turned the body over to view the face, hidden in the cowl, and suddenly recognized their former lord, although the years had not been kind.

Since then, when the moon is full and the village bell tolls the midnight hour, a cowled figure is sometimes seen wandering around the ruins. The people declare it is the ghost of Ulrich, the desecrater of his parents' tombs, who, in spite of pilgrimage and penance, cannot yet find any rest.

Andernach, *Heath's Picturesque Annual (1833)*

Laach
The Sunken Castle

The deep Lake of Laach, near Andernach on the Rhine, did not always exist. Tradition relates that a great hill once rose on this identical spot. On the topmost peak of this hill perched a mighty castle, the home of a wicked robber knight, the terror of all the country for many a mile around.

One day, this cruel Lord of Laach partook of a certain dish, which his cook declared was composed of nothing but stewed eels, but which, in reality, was a magical water snake. No sooner had he tasted it than he realized he could understand the language of beasts and birds. Imagine that! Wishing to keep this knowledge for himself alone, he ate up all there was in the dish. It happened, however, that the steward had tasted the broth in the pantry before he set in on his master's table. He, too, was able to understand the speech of animals just as cleverly as his master.

Although the Lord of Laach received such a fabulous gift, he was none the happier. All day long he listened to the animals criticize him for his cruelty. "A man should not hear such bitter truths about himself," he grumbled. Yet he did nothing to mend his ways. One day, however, he overheard the conversation of two hens.

"Have you heard the news?" cackled one.

"What news?" replied the other, scratching at the earth.

"Before sundown today the cruel Lord of Laach will sink along with his castle deep down into the earth."

"A fitting punishment," scorned the second hen. "He is a miserly and horrible creature."

"We best gather our chicks and fly away!" urged the first.

The Lord of Laach was horrified at this pronouncement. Hurrying to his stable, for it was nearly time for sunset, he hastily saddled his steed, snapping at his steward, "Bring out all of my most prized possessions immediately! All that I can carry!"

"What is it, sir?" The man clung to the bridle in terror, for he, too had understood the conversation of the chickens. "What doom have you brought on us? I beg you, my liege, bring me with you! I'm afraid to die!" But the cruel master struck him to the ground with his gauntleted fist.

Before he could ride out of the castle gate, however, the sun set and with a sudden rumbling noise the whole hill sank down into the bosom of the earth with the Lord of Laach and all his servants. When the astonished peasants visited the spot on the morrow, they found a lake rippling in the sunlight.

Many years after this terrible judgement, an island rose in the center of the lake. A little castle was built by order of another Lord of Laach, Helmut, a poet and musician who took great pleasure in life. The fairies, who are said to haunt the lake in great numbers, were so fond of this knight's music that one night, while he was sleeping, they gently drew island, castle and master down into the crystal depths of the lake. To this day, on quiet evenings when the moon is full, the soft sound of his lovely music can still be heard.

The Castle of Godesburg, *Heath's Picturesque Annual (1833)*

Andernach
The Baker Boys

During the Middle Ages, the inhabitants of Linz and Andernach could never agree and were continuously at war, each hoping to utterly destroy the other city. As the towns were only a short distance apart they could often pounce upon each other unaware.

The inhabitants of Linz, knowing the people of Andernach were sound sleepers, once resolved to attack them at dawn of day. In silence, the enemy stole up under the city wall and silently prepared to scale its heights. Their attempt would probably have proved successful had it not been for the greediness of two baker lads who had crept up into the tower to steal honey from the hives which the watchmen kept up there. Hearing a slight noise and fearing the approach of the watchmen, the youths cautiously peered over the wall and thus spied the enemy. A moment later, having thrown the hives down upon the foe, the boys rushed to the bell and loudly rang the alarm.

The Andernachers, springing out of bed, hurriedly donned their armor, seized their weapons and rushed out. But their presence was no longer necessary, as the infuriated bees had already routed the enemy.

In commemoration of this event, statues of the baker lads have been placed just within the Andernach gates. There they can still be seen, exact effigies of the boys who crept up the tower to steal honey and saved a town.

Niederwerth
The Divine Pilgrim

O n the long and beautiful island of Niederwerth, almost on the spot where the village of the same name now stands, there once rose a small convent which was inhabited by an abbess and twelve nuns. They were all remarkably holy women who spent all their time in prayer. The sisters were greatly terrified when a messenger brought news that Attila the Hun was drawing near with his band of marauders. Being heathens, they had no respect for the nun's sacred vows and were bound to treat them as cruelly as they would any other woman.

As there were no means of defense, and as their convent was remote from any settlement, the poor nuns could rely on no human aid. They prayed more fervently than ever that heaven have mercy upon them, and deliver them from the hands of their oppressors.

One evening when the midnight prayers were ended, the poor nuns were greatly startled by a noise at the door. When they discovered that it was only a poor pilgrim, they bade him welcome in the Lord's name, tenderly washed his weary feet, and compassionately gave him food and drink. After he was rested and refreshed, the pilgrim asked why the nuns were prolonging their vigils. "Is it normal at this house to pray after midnight?"

"We pray for our safety, good Pilgrim," spoke the abbess. "The Huns are on their way."

"You have helped me, dear Ladies, now let me advise you. Prepare thirteen coffins within the chapel, and when the foe approaches, let each sister commend her soul and body to God, and lie down in her coffin. I will be responsible for the rest."

The nuns, finding the advice good, on the morrow immediately prepared their coffins, and when the wild Huns appeared on the river bank, they withdrew to the chapel, recited the prescribed prayer, and calmly crossing their hands on their breasts, and lay down in their biers. As the outer doors fell in under the assailants ruthless blows, the aged pilgrim suddenly appeared in their midst and stretched out his hands in blessing over the reclining women. Their eyes closed, they assumed a livid, corpse-like hue, and soon appeared wan and shrunken like people long dead.

Two angels came in to light all the candles on the altar. When the Huns burst into the chapel they drew back appalled at the sight of the angelic host attending our Lord who, under the guise of an aged pilgrim, had come to defend the helpless nuns who had put all their trust in him. Filled with nameless dread, the Huns immediately reembarked in their frail skiffs and were overtaken by a storm, in which so many perished that the Rhine is said to have rolled corpses for many a day.

After the Huns' army had swept onward, survivors from the neighboring village crossed to the island to find how the nuns fared. They found the dormitory, refectory and chapel empty. Passing through the little churchyard, they found thirteen new graves within it, each bearing the name of one of the nuns, and the same date of death. But how they died, who carried them there, and who buried them remains a complete mystery.

Coblenz

St. Ritza

Louis I, the unworthy son of Charlemagne, is said to have lived for a time in Coblenz. His youngest daughter Ritza was born in Coblenz, and spent much of her early years in prayer. As soon as she was old enough to leave home, she obtained her father's permission to retire to a little hermitage on the other side of the Rhine on the spot where the Ehrenbreitstein fortress now stands.

To attend church, Ritza had to cross the Rhine River. As her faith was as pure as that of St. Peter, she fearlessly walked across the waters using no support except a slender willow twig. Of course, the rumor of this daily miracle soon attracted great attention. Each day a crowd gathered to watch her passage to-and-fro across the river. And each day, when the pious woman was safely across, they loudly extolled her virtues and called her a saint. This continued for many years.

The church bells were ringing loudly one stormy day and every wave was crested with a line of foam when Ritza came down to the shore as usual. For the first time the loud wind and dashing spray daunted her, and seeing a heavy staff lying near, the maiden took it instead of her willow wand. "Such a small wand would surely offer no support," she reasoned.

Somewhat hesitantly she now began her journey. When she reached the middle of the river she leaned heavily upon her staff, frightened by the threatening appearance of the white-capped waves, and immediately she began to sink. A moment later faith conquered. She flung the treacherous prop aside then clasped her hands, uttering a fervent prayer to heaven. She found herself able to stand upright once more in the midst of the heaving and tossing billows, through which she made her way safely to the opposite shore.

In gratitude for the timely aid she had received, Ritza resolved to place all her reliance, henceforth, in God alone, and daily crossed the tide without either wand or staff. When she died, the people bore her to St. Castor's church. There her tomb can still be seen. The people continue to revere her as a saint, and the Roman Catholics still lay offerings upon her shrine, imploring her aid in all cases of dire need.

Coblenz, *Heath's Picturesque Annual (1833)*

The Moselle Valley
St. Peter's Thirst

The valley of the Moselle, along whose winding course are dotted many medieval castles, was once visited by Christ and his disciples. Weary with the long journey and fainting from heat, He sat down by the roadside and bid St. Peter to hurry to the neighboring city of Coblenz and purchase a measure of wine for their refreshment.

Peter hurried to the city to purchase a sum of red wine. It was handed to him in a deep wooden measure such as they used in that part of the country. Without stopping to see the many fine sights the city had to offer, he immediately set out to return. Peter had not gone far, however, ere the wine began to run down over the sides of the vessel, which had been generously filled to the brim.

"Oh dear!" exclaimed Peter, "this will never, never do. It is a pity to lose any of this good wine. I had better drink a little so I can carry the measure without spilling any of its contents."

Peter, therefore, began to drink; but as he was hot and very thirsty, he took more than the sip he intended and when he raised his head, he saw with dismay that the measure no longer

Ruins of Thurant Castle

seemed full. Fearing lest he should be reproved for helping himself first, he quickly drew his knife out of his pocket and pared off a piece of the rim, so that the measure appeared as full as before. Then he continued on his way.

But soon the wine again began to overflow. He took another sip, which being also too great, forced him to use his knife a second time. Sipping and whittling, Peter thus continued his way, and when he at last came to the place where the Master and disciples were waiting for him, the measure, greatly reduced, contained barely enough wine to moisten their lips.

Silently the Master gazed upon Peter and then remarked dryly, "Peter, the next time you drink wine, be sure and wipe the drops away from your beard. But tell me, don't you think the people of this country must be very mean to sell their vintage in such miserable little things as these?" and He tapped the little wooden measure.

Peter hung his head and did not reply, but ever since then the wine measures along the Moselle, which are very small indeed, have been known as "miserabelchen," or miserable little things.

Thurant
A Carousing Army

The ruins of the ancient fortress of Thurant, which was built in 1200, tower above the Moselle and serve to remind travelers of the terrible siege that the castle endured during the middle ages. On one occasion, the united forces of the bishops of Trier and Cologne surrounded the stronghold, which was nobly defended by its owner. This knight and his brave garrison suffered much from hunger and thirst, while his foes drank their fill of fine Moselle wine. Many in the crowd hoped the castle would hold out "until they had emptied barrels enough to erect as imposing a building as the one they besieged."

This was before the days of gunpowder. Arrows and swords were of no avail when it was a question of seizing a well-defended castle, perched upon almost inaccessible heights, where battering rams and other ponderous war engines could not be used. To beguile the time the hosts of Trier and Cologne drank morning, noon and night. They laughed and caroused much to the exasperation of the garrison at Thurant, who had held out bravely for two whole years. During this time, the enemy drained no less than three thousand casks of Moselle wine.

The gatekeeper, weary of this long siege, longed to join in the noisy feasting which he saw daily. Finally he made secret arrangements to open the castle gates and deliver it into the enemy's hands. His treachery was discovered, and in punishment, his master ordered him to be tossed in a blanket from the top of the castle tower into the midst of the enemy's camp. Strange to relate, the gatekeeper landed unharmed in the midst of his foes, drank a long draught of wine from a skin pressed into his hand, and joined in the final siege. In gratitude for his narrow escape, he built the chapel on the Bleidenberg, from whence such a beautiful view can be obtained.

Stolzenfels
The Pet Raven

T he beautiful castle of Stolzenfels, which is now entirely
restored, was founded in the middle of the thirteenth century by Arnold von Isenburg, the Archbishop of Cleves. It was
later inhabited by Othmar and Willeswind, a brother and sister
who, having lost their parents, were devoted to each other and to
the care of their numerous retainers, who idolized them both.

The brother and sister were always together, so Willeswind
grieved sorely when Othmar was obliged to go off to war. He
took all the able-bodied men with him, and left none but the old
men, women and children at home. As there were many lawless
robber knights along the Rhine in those days, Willeswind wisely
ordered that the castle gates should remain closed. She sallied
forth only at midday to visit a few of her pensioners in the village, and to say a prayer for her brother in the village church.

One evening, while she was sitting in the hall with all her retainers, the women busily at work spinning and the men burnishing
their arms, the warder suddenly came to announce the presence
of a pilgrim begging for shelter. "Admit him immediately,"
Willeswind declared. "And bring him a bowl of hot soup."

In spite of the pilgrim's worn garments, he inspired the maiden
with a vague feeling of fear. His face was both cunning and cruel,
and his roving glances seemed to take note of the castle defenses
and of the small number of her aged retainers. Her suspicions,
which were shared by the warder, were only too soon justified.

Although the pilgrim departed peaceably on the morrow, he
came back three days later in full armor. In a cold and cruel voice he
said, "Willeswind, my love, I have come for your hand in marriage."

"Marry you?" she scorned. "I'd rather die."

"Oh my dear, unless you consent in three days' time, I shall be forced to take you by means of violence."

Willeswind sighed in resignation. She knew it would be impossible for her aged retainers to hold out against the robber knight's forces. It was not worth the loss of their lives. "Give me three days, as you promised," she said firmly. "I will give you an answer then."

When the knight withdrew, she immediately had one of her retainers dispatch a message to Othmar. "Until your brother can come to your aid, my Lady, I suggest you retire to a convent," urged her warder.

"I agree," she said grimly, and ordered a trunk to be packed. On her way to the abbey with only a small escort, Willeswind fell into an ambush laid by the treacherous knight.

"You thought to outwit me?" he laughed. "How noble. But as you can see, worthless."

He soon overcame Willeswind's brave retainers, made her captive, and carried her off with her maid to a lonely tower in the woods. There he locked them both in, declaring "I will come back in three days' time, my Lady, and I expect a favorable answer to my suit."

As soon as he had departed, Willeswind and her maid began to inspect the premises. Try as they might, they could devise no means of escape, for the walls were thick, doors and windows heavily barred and, in spite of careful search, they could find neither water nor food.

"It is hopeless," said the maid. "This tower is in the wilderness. Who will come to lend us aid?"

"Wait!" Willeswind interrupted. "There is hope." She pointed excitedly and whistled to her pet raven, circling high overhead. "What are you doing here little bird?" she smiled happily. "Did you think to seek me out?"

She had trained this bird to bring her berries, and she knew her faithful raven would be able to feed them. She sent the bird back into the wind and watched as it journeyed busily to-and-fro, bringing so many luscious berries that Willeswind and her maid did not suffer from either hunger or thirst.

Three days later the robber knight appeared, greatly surprised when Willeswind rejected his addresses as haughtily as ever. "Hmm," he said. "You are made of stronger mettle than I imagined. No matter. Another three days in the tower will make you more agreeable."

Time passed very slowly in that gloomy prison. In spite of the raven's visits, the girls were very faint and weak, and on the third day, while eagerly watching for the bird's return, Willeswind suddenly saw a knight emerge from the thicket and ride by. Judging by his horse and armor that it could not be her ravisher, she called aloud for aid and wildly waved her handkerchief through the bars.

The knight turned and Willeswind recognized her brother. Before he could take any measures to deliver her, however, the robber knight came riding up the overgrown path. Seeing Othmar, he challenged him to a fight. "For your castle and your sister!" he shouted.

Othmar, furious at the man's insolent behavior and the heartache he had made poor Willeswind endure, fought so bravely that he soon sent his antagonist lifeless to the ground. He seized the keys from his belt and freed the captives who had languished nearly a week in the tower.

As Othmar and Willeswind slowly rode away, the raven, returning with a host of its companions, swooped down upon the robber knight's corpse and pecked out the eyes. Willeswind, safe home once more in her beloved Stolzenfels, now recounted all her adventures to her brother, who ordered an effigy of the raven to be placed above the gateway to commemorate the fidelity of the pet bird whose exertions had preserved two human lives.

Marksburg
The Murdered Wife

The fortress of Marksburg, the only old fortress along the Rhine which has remained in a perfect state of preservation, is almost impregnable. This castle once belonged to Ludwig the Cruel, Lord of Braubach, who married a young and beautiful, but weak-minded woman called Mariah. As she found it impossible to love her husband, this faithless wife began a flirtation with a steward called Henry, who was passionately in love with her. Ludwig, however, soon discovered this state of affairs and knew how to quickly put it to an end. He needed to leave home on business and asked Henry to accompany him. "It would take a miracle to keep that relationship going," he thought with satisfaction. But, in spite of all his vigilance, Mariah and Henry managed to exchange many a letter through the lady's maid. They would have escaped detection had not Mariah made the mistake of sending a letter intended for her lover to her husband.

Ludwig the Cruel, finding he had been outwitted, was so furious that he rode straight home. The household was in an uproar to see their lord riding so unexpectedly up the road. When he reached the gates, he ordered that the maid who had acted as go-between be tossed out of the window onto the rocks beneath the castle. Then, accompanied by two executioners, he entered his wife's room and had her beheaded without further ado. This singularly evil deed was greatly resented by Ludwig's people. Doubtless they would have punished him for his cruelty had they not been so afraid of him. And so they let him be.

Although avenged, Ludwig was far from happy. He was tormented by such keen remorse that he did penance for his sins and founded a nunnery which was named in honor of the wife whom he had so mercilessly slain.

Dinkhold Fountain
The Spectral Foot

In a little valley, not far from Braubach, are the mineral springs known as the Dinkhold, the favorite haunt of a nymph named Aegle, daughter of old Father Rhine.

Many years ago a young knight lived at the head of this little valley. Daily he rode down it with his mounted train on his way to the Rhine or to the chase. On one occasion he was detained, and sending his followers ahead of him, presently rode down the familiar valley alone. Imagine his surprise when he saw a fountain in a spot which had hitherto been dry and arid. His amazement doubled at the sight of an ethereal maiden bending gracefully over the fountain. This creature proved so attractive that he immediately dismounted. Going to her, he asked her name and how she came to be here.

He soon learned who she was, declared the love which had been kindled at the first sight of her, and was overjoyed when she confessed that she had long loved him, and had only waited for him to pass by alone to reveal herself to him.

Aegle, the beautiful nymph, in spite of her protestations of affection was very shy, indeed, and erelong told her lover she must depart. "Meet me here on the morrow," she said and vanished before he could utter a protest or try to detain her.

The knight was, of course, faithful to his appointment on the morrow. Yet when he would fain have embraced the timid Aegle, she shrank back, "Nay, sir! I must go. I will meet you on the morrow. But if by that time you have not learned to behave as a true and loyal knight, I will never come again."

She vanished as soon as this speech was ended and the knight went home in confusion. All night long, he cudgeled his brain to find out what her mysterious words might mean. It was only as the dawn approached that he realized he spoke countless words of love, but had never once mentioned the subject of marriage. His first words on the morrow, therefore, would be to ask Aegle when she would become his wife, and to persuade her to meet him in his castle chapel that evening and plight her troth to him there at the altar.

Aegle, whose beautiful face grew radiant at these words, promised to do so. "But I would be a poor wife indeed if I did not warn you that marriage to a nymph is dangerous."

"How dangerous could it be?" he laughed at the young and graceful maiden.

"You will lose your life if ever you become faithless."

The knight was sure of his love, and led her to the altar where they were married. For seven years he lived with the beautiful Aegle, who was a devoted wife and bore him several lovely children. The happiness of this married couple was troubled at last by rumors of war. Aegle shed her first tears when her husband was obliged to join the imperial army. She clung to him imploring him, "Do not for a moment forget about me. Faithlessness will be punished by death." They parted beside the fountain where they had first met, and Aegle returned home to watch for her beloved's return.

After many months of warfare, peace was concluded. The Emperor Henry, wishing to reward the knight for his bravery, summoned him into his presence and proposed to give him the hand of his beautiful niece, Agnes, who had long loved him in secret. With as much dignity as possible, the knight declared, "That is an honor far too great for so humble a subject as myself. And, as I am already married, I am forbidden to enter into any other alliance."

Angry and disappointed at this refusal, Henry questioned him closely. When he heard that the knight had married a nymph, he crossed himself and shouted for the bishop. "I beg you, your eminence, convince this knight of the sin he has committed in loving a faerie. Tell this man that he must annul such an unholy contract. Then he will be free to marry my niece."

The bishop, who was a subtle reasoner, argued with the knight. He so bewildered the poor young man that the knight finally agreed to marry the fair Agnes. But when the ceremony was over, and the wedding guests were seated around for the festal board, the knight's eyes suddenly dilated with horror. There, floating in the air before him, was a small, white, naked foot. In the presence of all the guests, it kicked him before it vanished.

Crying out, "Aegle!" the knight fell down unconscious. Vainly Agnes tried to revive him, but the bishop, who was versed in magic, declared "He must be carried over the Rhine. Running water is part of the wild magic, subject to neither good nor evil, and it will break the hold these foul spirits have over him."

The attendants immediately carried the knight down to a boat. Many of the guests followed as well, but when they reached the middle of the river, a great wave swept suddenly down upon them, dashing over the boat and carrying away the knight's body. The faithless man was never seen again. One of the boatmen, however, declared that he saw a little white foot kicking the knight under the waters, and heard the unhappy knight again cry, "Aegle!"

The emperor's niece Agnes, having lost her bridegroom, withdrew to a neighboring convent where she spent the remainder of her life as a nun. As to Aegle, the rightful wife? No one knows for sure. On the very day when the knight perished, Aegle and her children vanished. At the same time, the waters of the Dinkhold fountain suddenly turned bitter to the taste, and have never again been sweet as at first, although they are considered a sure cure for every complaint except a broken heart.

Katzenellenbogen
The Assassin Priest

The castle of Katzenellenbogen, which is generally known as "The Cat," was built in the fourteenth century. It was once occupied by a very popular lord and his equally unpopular wife. She was greatly disliked on account of her horrid behavior.

Worn out by her constant nagging, her husband finally obtained a divorce. As he had no children to inherit his vast possessions, he soon married again, choosing this time a lady as lovable, gentle and good as she was pretty. In the course of his wedding journey, he led his bride to his castle of Rheinfels, where a priest, hired by his divorced wife to kill her hated rival, administered a subtle poison in the communion cup to the maiden.

The countess, noticing the powder on the wine, called the priest's attention to it. "Ah, my Lady, drink it without fear. It is nothing but a little dust which has fallen from the ceiling." The young bride obeyed, and was soon seized with convulsions. Although she did not die, her health was permanently impaired. She would never be able to bear any children.

Soon after, the Count of Katzenellenbogen also became mysteriously ill and died, leaving all his possessions to the noble house of Hesse, for he had no direct heir.

The priest's crimes were eventually discovered, and after a public ceremony in which all the emblems of his sacred office were solemnly taken from him, he was deposed from the priestly office and hanged amid the loud cheers of the assembled people. As for the first wife, we do not know what happened to her, for the annals of history are strangely silent on this matter.

Thurnberg
The Bell in the Well

The ruins of the ancient castle of Thurnberg tower above the little village of Welmich, not very far from St. Goar. This castle was called "The Mouse" by the haughty lords of Katzenellenbogen, for their stronghold was known as "The Cat," and they openly boasted far and wide that their cat would soon devour the mouse. But for all their boasting, it never did so, and the little mouse ever kept them at bay.

Above the ruins of The Mouse, lights are often seen after sunset. The people declare they are the reflections of the fire in which a former owner, an evil man, is slowly burning in the Infernal Regions.

Tradition relates that, irritated by the ringing of the village church bell, which on Sunday mornings always roused him from his nap, this nobleman had it confiscated. When the priest came to claim it, the Lord of Thurnberg had the bell bound firmly round the priest's neck, and ordered him flung into a very deep well in the courtyard.

The clang of the bell was not silenced by this crime. The deeper it fell the louder it pealed, waking all the echoes with its deafening sound. The bell rang loudly night and day, finally driving Lord Thurnberg mad. Unable to stand it a moment longer, he leaped into the well, falling to his death. The moment he had breathed his last, the bell suddenly ceased ringing.

Since that time the bell has been heard each midnight, on the 18th of January, the anniversary of the wicked Lord of Thurnberg's death.

Bacharach
Barbarossa's Beard

F rederick Barbarossa, emperor of Germany, was the owner of a magnificent, fiery red beard. The devil coveted it sorely, and told his minions, "Wouldn't such a fine beard complement a gentleman of my rosy complexion? Isn't it delicately suggestive of the flames of hell?"

As the devil was unable to grow a beard of his own, he finally decided to steal Barbarossa's. Never having had the need to shave, and not knowing how to proceed, he traveled to the little town of Bacharach on the Rhine to engage the services of one of the town's numerous barbers.

"I'll shave off Barbarossa's beard," said one of the barbers. "But I want something from you in return."

"Name your price," said the devil, always in the mood for a good bargain.

"It is unlikely that Barbarossa will sit still while I shave his whiskers. I need you to guarantee that he will not kill me where I stand."

"I will transport you safely to the palace," said the devil. "And I'll cause a deep sleep to fall upon the emperor." And so it was decided.

A faerie, overhearing this plan and knowing that Frederick would visit Bacharach a few days later, wished to protect him from the devil's plot. The emperor had once done her a good turn, and she longed to return the favor. So this faerie went in search of a giant, and coaxed him to lend her his great beard. The giant squinted down at the tiny faerie. "You'll be crushed by the weight of my beard if you try to carry it in your sack. Let me go with you, we will shave it in Bacharach." Walking side by side they came to the entrance of the city, just as the town clocks were striking twelve.

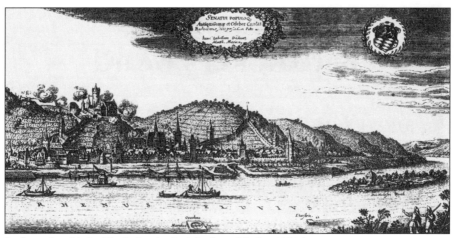

Bacharach with Stahleck Castle, *by Matthäus Merian (1645)*

"Sit here," said the faerie. "I won't be long." She sprinkled faerie dust into the eyes of all the town's barbers so that they would not wake up. By means of magic she then stuffed them all into her sack, including the one who promised to aid Satan. She decided rather than risk fooling the devil with a false beard, she would instead rid the village of its barbers.

"Get up!" she said to the giant who had fallen into a doze. "I need you to carry this sack to the edge of the Rhine and toss it into its depths."

The giant shouldered his burden and tramped off. The barbers, awakened by the jolting, kicked and struggled to get out of the sack. They frightened the giant so much that he ran as quickly as he could to the river and tossed the bag far out into the middle. Some people say that the barbers all drowned that day; others say that they live beneath the waves still, the guests of Father Rhine.

When Frederick Barbarossa arrived in Bacharach, the devil could only stare in envy and frustration at the emperor's fiery red beard. There was not a single barber left in town to come to his aid.

St. Goar
Godfather Death

There was once a poor man of St. Goar who had twelve children, and he was obliged to labor day and night that he might earn food for them. When at length, as it so happened, a thirteenth came into the world. The poor man did not know how to help himself, so he ran out into the highway, determined to ask the first person he met to be godfather to the boy. There came stalking up to him Death, who said, "Take me as godfather."

"Who are you?" asked the father.

"I am Death, who makes all equal," replied the stranger.

Then the man said, "You are of the right sort. You seize on rich and poor without distinction. You shall be the child's godfather."

Death answered, "I will make the boy rich and renowned throughout the world, for he who has me for a friend can want nothing."

"Next Sunday he will be christened," said the man. "Be sure to arrive on time."

Death accordingly appeared as he had promised, and stood godfather to the child. When the boy grew up, his godfather came to him one day, and took him into a wood, and said, "Now you shall have your godfather's present. I will make a most famous physician of you. Whenever you are called to a sick person, I will take care and show myself to you. If I stand at the foot of the bed, say boldly, 'I will soon restore you to health,' and give the patient a little herb that I will point out to you, and he will soon be well. If, however, I stand at the head of the sick person, he is mine. Say, 'All help is useless. He must soon die.'" Then Death showed him the little herb, saying, "Take heed that you never use it in opposition to my will."

It was not long before the young fellow was the most celebrated physician in all of Germany. The people of St. Goar would boast of his skills to all who would listen, "The moment he sees a person, he knows whether or not he'll recover." Accordingly he was soon in great demand. People came from far and near to consult him, and they gave him whatever he required, so that he made an immense fortune.

Now, it so happened that the Lord of Bacharach was taken ill, and the physician was called upon to say whether he must die. As he went up to the bed, he saw Death standing at the sick man's head, so that there was no chance of his recovery. The physician thought, however, that if he outwitted his godfather just this once, he would not, perhaps, be much offended. So he caught hold of the knight and turned him round, so that by that means Death was standing at his feet. Then he gave him some of the herb, and the knight recovered, and was once more well. Death came up to the physician with a very angry and gloomy countenance, and said, "I will forgive what you have done this time, because I am your godfather, but if you ever venture to betray me again, you must take the consequences."

Soon after this, Lord Bacharach's daughter fell sick, and nobody could cure her. The old knight wept night and day, until his eyes were blinded, and at last he proclaimed that whosoever rescued her from Death should be rewarded by marrying her and inheriting the castle.

The physician came, but Death was standing at the head of the princess. When the physician saw the beauty of the knight's daughter, and thought of the promise that the good Lord had made, he forgot all the warnings he had received and, although Death frowned heavily all the while, he turned the patient so that Death stood at her feet. He gave her some of the herb, so that he once more put life into her veins.

When Death saw that he was a second time cheated out of his property, he stepped up to the physician and said, "Now, Godson, I want you to follow me."

76

He laid hold of him with his icy cold hand, and led him into a subterranean cave, in which there were thousands and thousands of burning candles, arranged in innumerable rows. Some were whole, some half burnt out, while fresh ones were lit so that the little flames seemed perpetually hopping about.

"Behold," said death. "The life candles of mankind. The large ones belong to children, those half consumed to middle aged people, the little ones to the aged. Yet children and young people have oftentimes but a little candle, and when that is burned out, their life is at an end, and they are mine."

The physician said in a shaky voice, "Show me my candle."

Then Death pointed out a very little candle end, which was glimmering in the socket and said, "That is yours."

"Oh, Godfather! Light me up a new one, that I may first enjoy my life, be Lord of Bacharach, and husband to the beautiful maiden your herbs restored!"

"I cannot do so," said Death, shaking his head. "One must burn out before I can light another."

"Place the old one then upon a new one that that may burn on when this is at an end," said the physician.

Death pretended that he would comply with this wish, and reached for a large, fat candle. But to revenge himself he purposefully failed in lighting it, and the little stub of his godson's candle sputtered and went out. The physician sank with it, himself falling into the hands of Death.

Lorelei
The Unhappy Beauty

The bed of the Rhine grows suddenly narrow and almost fathomless after St. Goar. Great masses of rock rise high into the sky, shutting out the pleasant light of the sun. On the right bank, a huge basaltic cliff towers over the waters. This is the famous Loreleiberg, noted for its magnificent views, its seven-fold echo, and for the numerous romantic legends connected with it. The most famous is of the beautiful Lorelei.

Lorelei lived in Bacharach on the Rhine at the beginning of the eleventh century. Suitors without end came to woo her, and because she was as tender-hearted as she was beautiful, she saw the misery her loveliness inflicted. Gladly would she have consented to lose all her charms could she have saved anyone from pain.

Then Lorelei herself fell in love with a handsome young knight of the neighborhood. The young people always met in secret, so no one knew of their love or their betrothal until war was declared in the land. "I must leave you now, my pretty Lorelei, to win honor and glory before claiming you as my wife." Vainly she entreated him to remain by her side; vainly she pictured the dangers and possible death which awaited him, but he refused to listen to anything save the promptings of his ambition.

Lorelei no longer took any pleasure in life. In spite of her openly announced engagement, new suitors constantly crowded around her, trying to win her from her allegiance to her absent lover. Although no tidings of the rover reached her—good news or bad—she feared he had either perished or turned faithless. She was convinced he was not coming back.

Despite her convictions, however, she still refused to console herself with the love of another. Every day some new suitor appeared, and every day the village gossips whispered that some rejected lover had drowned himself in the Rhine, pined to death, or left the country to find an honorable end on the battle-field. Only a few youths were now left in the country, and every-one knew they were well and happy only because they had never seen the beautiful Lorelei, and that as soon as their eyes rested upon her they too would fall victims to her charms. Mothers with marriageable daughters were specially anxious to get rid of Lorelei and, little by little, spread the dark report that it was not only the maiden's beauty which won the hearts of men, but her magic arts, spells, and incantations. The rumor, as rumors will, spread so rapidly that Lorelei was finally summoned to appear before the criminal court of the archbishop of Cologne.

There, in spite of all accusations made by vicious gossips, judge and jury alike agreed that such a beautiful, innocent face could not belong to a guilty person, and acquitted her. Lorelei, feeling that life had no charms for her, and weary of persecution, now flung herself at the archbishop's feet, crying, "I'm not a witch, but let me die! I'm so unhappy. My lover has forsaken me and his silence has lasted so long that I am sure he is either faith-less or dead. Life is a burden to me, for the young men of the neighborhood constantly annoy me by pleading for a love which I cannot give, as my heart is in my lover's keeping. Let me die!"

The aged prelate kindly raised the tearful child and said, "My dear Lorelei, I see no cause to credit the accusations against you. I see no evidence that you are a practitioner of magical arts. I see, only too plainly, the natural charms which have done so much harm through no fault of your own. I cannot let you die. But, if you wish to mourn in peace, you may enter a convent, where none will ever again bother you."

Lorelei accepted this proposal with joy. Two old knights were summoned to escort her to her future home, and the little caval-cade wended its way along the Rhine, and crossed it at St. Goar. Soon after they drew near a huge mass of basaltic rock, which Lorelei expressed to climb, so that she "might view her home once more." The old knights immediately agreed to this innocent request, and the maiden, bounding lightly ahead, climbed until she reached the highest point and stood directly above the dark stream. Her tearful eyes rested for a moment on her native town then upon the towers of her lover's home, and lastly fell upon a boat slowly floating down the stream. At the sight of a mailed figure standing at the helm, she suddenly uttered a loud cry of joy, for she recognized the lover whom she had long believed dead. Her sudden exclamation, rousing the echoes, attracted the attention of the knight who, still faithful, forgot all else at the sight of his beloved standing far above him with outstretched arms.

The little boat, no longer guided by the helm, was seized by the current, whirled against the dangerous rocks, and dashed to pieces. Lorelei, seeing her lover's danger, made as if to save him, lost her balance, and fell over the precipice into the Rhine, where she perished by his side at the foot of the rock which still bears her name.

Untitled Image from Rheinsagen by Karl d'Efter

Lorelei
The Fisherman

Another tradition of the Lorelei which, although equally tragic, differs widely in many points from the first, has inspired Heine's immortal song, still sung along the Rhine, and is generally told as follows:

Long years ago, whenever the moonlight flooded mountains and river, a beautiful maiden was seen seated upon the top of the Lorelei rock. There she sang sweet and entrancing melodies while she combed her long golden hair with a jeweled comb; her pure white draperies fluttered in the night winds as she made her toilet under the blue vault of heaven and by the witching light of the moon.

This fair creature, whom all called Lorelei, was an immortal, a water nymph, daughter of old Father Rhine. During the day, she lingered in the cool depths of the river bed, but late at night she sat aloft where travelers and boatmen could easily see her, but woe unto them if the evening breeze wafted the notes of her song to their ears! The entrancing melody made each one forget time and place until their vessels, no longer guided along the dangerous pass, were whirled against the rocks where they were dashed to pieces, and all on board perished. There bodies would be found later, a smile on their cold features.

One person only is said to have been favored with a near view of the charming Lorelei. A handsome young fisherman from Oberwesel climbed the rocks every evening to spend a few delightful hours with the river nymph, his head pillowed in her lap, his eyes drinking in her beauty, his ears charmed by the melody of her song.

Tradition further relates that ere they parted the Lorelei invariably pointed out the places where he was to cast his nets on the morrow, and as he always carried out her instructions, he never came home with an empty creel.

One moonlight night the fisherman was seen as usual boldly scaling the rocks to keep his tryst, but he never came down the cliff again. The river was dragged, the rock was searched, but no trace of him was found. The people of the surrounding villages declare that Lorelei dragged him down into her crystal palace beneath the flood to enjoy his society undisturbed forever.

Loreleyfelsen, *Das Blaue Buch vom Rhein*

Lorelei
A Magic Spell

C ount Ludwig, the only son of Prince Palatine, once left his father's castle at Stalheck to sail down the Rhine, hoping to catch a glimpse of the siren Lorelei of whom he had often heard such marvelous tales. It was evening. The stars were twinkling softly overhead as his boat slowly drifted down the river. Darker and darker grew the waters as the bed of the Rhine grew narrower, but the young count paid no heed to that. His eyes were fixed on the rocks far above, where he hoped to catch sight of the beautiful nymph.

Suddenly he saw a glimmer of white drapery and golden hair and heard the faint, sweet sound of an alluring song. As he drew nearer, the melody became more distinct and the moonbeams falling upon the maiden seemed to enhance her marvelous beauty as she bent over the rocky ledge beckoning to Ludwig to draw near. The count and boatmen, spellbound by the vision above them, paid little heed to their vessel until it was too late. Striking against the rocks, it sunk with nearly all on board. Only one escaped to tell of the young count's cruel fate. The maiden, high above, continued her song.

The bereaved father, thirsting for revenge, issued immediate orders for the capture of the siren who had caused so much woe. Several of his most seasoned warriors set out at the head of an armed band, which they posted all around the rock with strict orders not to let the nymph escape. Then, climbing noiselessly up the moonlit cliff, the captain and three of his men suddenly presented themselves before the matchless Lorelei. She was, as usual, combing her hair and crooning her song. The men hemmed her in so securely that no mode of escape remained except straight down to the river. "Surrender now, witch," the captain demanded.

Quite unmoved, however, the nymph gracefully waved her white hands and whispered a few words onto the wind. The grim old warriors were suddenly rooted to the spot, utterly incapable of moving hand or foot or of uttering the slightest sound. With fear-widened eyes fixed upon the Lorelei, they saw her remove her jewels, dropping them one by one into the Rhine at her feet. Then she whirled about in mystic dance, muttering some strange spell. The only words the captain and his men could make out had to do with "white-maned steeds and a pearl shell chariot." When dance and song were ended, the waters of the Rhine suddenly began to bubble and seethe, and rose higher and higher, until they reached the top of the cliff. The petrified warriors felt the cold tide surge about their feet. Suddenly they saw a great white-crested wave rolling rapidly toward them, and in its green depths they beheld a chariot drawn by white-maned steeds. Lorelei sprang into this carriage, and quickly vanished over the edge of the cliff, into the river.

A moment later the angry waters subsided; the men recovered the power of motion, and when they bent down over the cliff, no trace of the sudden flood could be seen except for the water drops, shining in the moonlight like diamonds along the face of the cliff.

The next morning Count Ludwig's body was found washed ashore near the Pfalz, somehow finding its way contrary to the course of the current. It was doubtless borne there by the Lorelei, who has never again reappeared on the cliff, although boatmen and belated travelers have often heard the faint sweet echo of her alluring song, wafted toward them on the summer breeze at midnight.

Schönberg
The Seven Sisters

In the castle of Schönberg, whose ruins tower above the little town of Oberwesel, there once dwelt seven beautiful girls. They were sisters, and as they had no living relative they exercised full control over their persons, lands and fortunes.

As these young ladies were so very attractive, they were wooed by knights of every degree. Although they delighted in receiving attentions — and what maiden wouldn't? — they would never consent to bind themselves by any vows. They favored a suitor for a short time, merely for the pleasure of watching his impotent wrath when discarded to make room for a rival. One knight after another thus left the castle in despair. But for every one who departed discouraged, two arrived full of hope, confident in their powers to please and hold the capricious fair.

One day a Minnesinger arrived at Schönberg and fell desperately in love with Adelgunde, the youngest sister. For her he composed his sweetest lays, sung to the accompaniment of his guitar. Day after day the maiden led him on, making him believe her heart was all his own, but in reality caring nothing for him. She took careful note of all his passionate speeches, only to report them to her sisters and make fun of the enamored youth.

Anxious to witness one of the love scenes she described so vividly, the six other sisters concealed themselves in various parts of the apartment, leaving Adelgunde apparently alone. A few moments later the Minnesinger appeared and, finding his lady love unchaperoned, fell upon his knees before her and eloquently declared his love. While he was still pleading with eager eyes and trembling lips for the love he thought he had won, the sisters rushed out of their hiding places and began to mimic him, while Adelgunde, whom he had fancied so gentle, noble and refined, laughed louder than all the rest at his discomfiture.

Enraged at this heartless treatment, the Minnesinger rushed out of the castle, sprang on his horse, galloped madly down the steep hill and, beside himself with grief, plunged into the Rhine. There tradition relates that the water nymphs laid him on a soft couch in their crystal palace and bade him confide all his sorrows to their queen, the matchless golden-haired Lorelei. When he had told her the story of his love and despair, she exclaimed, "Many are the complaints which have reached my ears about those cold-hearted maidens. I swear to you that just punishment will soon overtake them. Sweet minstrel, sorrow and care shall never again approach your poetic soul. Tune your guitar and forget you were once unhappy. You shall remain here with me."

The Lorelei then gently waved her faerie wand. At the same moment the pain in the Minnesinger's heart vanished; his sorrows were forgotten; his eye beamed with happiness, and his guitar awoke to a joyful lay beneath the touch of his inspired fingers. When she saw him happy once more, the Lorelei left her crystal palace and went in search of the cruel ladies of Schönberg whom she had resolved to punish.

It was one of those matchless summer evenings along the Rhine, and the sisters were idly drifting down the stream in their tiny boat, talking and laughing incessantly. While they were, as usual, recounting their heartless triumphs and mimicking their unfortunate suitors, the Lorelei suddenly rose out of the waves before them and solemnly warned, "Your end is near."

In vain the frivolous sisters pleaded for mercy; in vain they proffered their richest gifts. The Lorelei insisted that as they had shown no compassion for the sufferings of others, they need expect no reprieve, and while she was still speaking, the vessel suddenly sank with all its living freight.

On the morrow, seven rocks rose out of the river in a spot where none had previously stood, and the superstitious aver that these are the bodies of the seven sisters, which have become as hard as their hearts. On stormy evenings, they say, their drowning shrieks rise above the sound of the wind and waves.

Lorch
Peter Klaus

Peter Klaus, a goatherd of Lorch, tended herds near the Wisperthal Valley. He used to let them rest of an evening in a spot surrounded by an old wall, where he always counted them to see if they were all right. For some days he noticed that one of his finest goats, as they came to this spot, vanished. It never returned to the herd until quite late. He watched more closely, and at length saw the beast slip through a rent in the wall.

Peter followed the goat, and caught him in a cave, feeding on the grains of oats which fell one by one from the roof. He looked up, shook his head at the shower of oats, but could discover nothing more. At length he heard the neighing and stamping of some mettlesome horses overhead, and concluded that the oats must have fallen from their mangers.

While the goatherd stood there, wondering about these horses in a totally uninhabited mountain, a lad came and made signs to him to follow him silently. Peter ascended some steps and, crossing a walled court, came to a glade surrounded by rocky cliffs into which a sort of twilight made its way through the thick-leaved branches. Here he found twelve grave old knights playing at skittles at a well-leveled and fresh plot of grass. Peter was silently appointed to set up the ninepins for them.

At first his knees knocked together as he did this, while he marked, with half-stolen glances, the long beards and goodly paunches of the noble knights. By degrees, however, he grew more confident, and looked at everything about him with a steady gaze—nay, at last, he ventured so far as to take a draught from a pitcher which stood near him, the fragrance of which appeared to him delightful. He felt quite revived by the draught, and as often as he felt at all tired, received new strength from application to the inexhaustible pitcher, but at length sleep overcame him.

⌒

When he awoke, he found himself once more in the enclosed green space, where he was accustomed to leave his goats. He rubbed his eyes, but could discover neither dog nor goats, and stared with surprise at the height to which the grass had grown, and the bushes and trees, which he never remembered to have noticed. Shaking his head, he proceeded along the roads and paths which he was accustomed to traverse daily with his herd, but could nowhere see any traces of his goats. Below him he saw Lorch, and at last he descended with quickened step.

The people whom he met at his entrance to the town were unknown to him and dressed and spoke differently from those whom he had known there. Moreover, they all stared at him when he inquired about his goats, and began stroking their chins. At last, almost involuntarily, he did the same, and found, to his great astonishment, that his beard had grown to be a foot long. He began now to think himself and the world altogether bewitched, and yet he felt sure that the mountains from which he had descended were the same as those that overshadowed the Rhine, and the houses here, with their fore-courts, were all familiar to him. Moreover, several lads whom he heard telling the name of the place to a traveller called it Lorch.

Shaking his head, he proceeded into the town straight to his own house. He found it sadly fallen to decay. Before it lay a strange herd-boy in tattered garments, and near him an old worn-out dog, which growled and showed his teeth at Peter when he called him. He entered by the opening, which had formerly been closed by a door, but found all within so desolate and empty that he staggered out again like a drunkard, and called his wife and children. No one heard. No voice answered him.

Women and children now began to surround the strange old man with his long, hoary beard, and to contend with one another in inquiring of him what he wanted. He thought it so ridiculous to make inquiries of strangers, before his own house, after his wife and children, and still more so, after himself, that he mentioned the first neighbor whose name occurred to him, Kurt Stiffen. All were silent and looked at one another, till an old woman said, "He has left here these twelve years. He lives in Sachsenberg. You'll hardly get there today."

"Velten Maier?"

"God help him!" said an old crone leaning on a crutch. "He has been confined these fifteen years in the house, which he'll never leave again."

He recognized, as he thought, his suddenly aged neighbor, but he had lost all desire of asking any more questions. At last a brisk young woman, with a boy of twelve months old in her arms and a little girl holding her hand, made her way through the gaping crowd. They looked for all the world like his wife and children.

"What is your name?" asked Peter, astonished.

"Maria."

"And your father?"

"God have mercy on him, it is Peter Klaus. It is twenty years since we sought him day and night in the mountains, when his goats came home without him. I was only seven years old when it happened."

The goatherd could no longer contain himself. "I am Peter Klaus!" he cried. "I and no other!" And he took the babe from his daughter's arms.

All stood like statues for a minute, till one and then another began to cry, "Here's Peter Klaus come back again! Welcome, welcome, neighbor, after twenty years! Welcome Peter Klaus!"

Sonneck
The Ghost Feast

The castle of Sonneck, with its tall tower, was first built in 1015 and was the ancestral home of a noble family of the same name. All of the men of this race were remarkably fond of hunting in their wide forests, and the castle eventually fell into the hands of Prince Heinrich, who loved the chase so dearly that it absorbed all his time and thoughts.

To be perfectly free to indulge in his favorite pastime, the young Lord of Sonneck entrusted all his business to the care of a steward. This man sorely oppressed all the poor people, but Heinrich always exclaimed that he had no time to hear their complaints. His only interest was to travel in the woods and hunt.

One day, however, he could start no game, so he proposed that he and his companions should separate and scour the forest in different directions, returning to meet again at nightfall. They each went their own way, and Prince Heinrich soon started a stag which he hotly pursued, only to see it vanish mysteriously after a long run. Only then did he look around to establish his bearings, and was greatly surprised to find himself in a stretch of forest he never before had hunted. Although he repeatedly blew his horn, no answering sound was heard. He was about to ride on when he spied a gaunt, cadaverous-looking form rise before him, and heard a voice command him in sepulchral tones, to follow.

Involuntarily Prince Heinrich obeyed. As he passed on he noticed with awe that the garments of his guide seemed covered with mold and that he exhaled an ancient and earth-like smell. A few moments later they came before a building which Heinrich had never seen. He dismounted and followed his guide into a great hall. There he saw a long table, on either side of which were seated many ghastly-looking guests who silently devoured the rich food set before them. They seemed to swallow it with grimaces of pain. When he had gazed for several minutes upon this strange feast, the guide grabbed hold of his sleeve and led him back to the place where he had first seen him.

The strange guide paused for a moment, studying the prince carefully. Then he said, "Those guests to the feast were your ancestors. Each is condemned to eat the food which, in spite of its delicious appearance and aroma, is as bitter as the apples of Sodom. This is the punishment inflicted upon them for their selfish absorption in their own pleasures. Be warned, oh Prince," he concluded, "for our life is unbearable and our hearts constantly burn hot within us."

With these words, the specter pushed aside the damp folds of his moldly garments and there, between his whitening ribs, the count saw a glowing ball of fire. A moment later the apparition vanished and Heinrich, looking in the direction of the palace, saw only a raging sea of flames, which slowly sank down to the earth. The horror of the heart-rending cries and groans heard from within made his hair stand up on end.

When the count of Sonneck arrived home that evening, his servants were surprised to find that his coal black hair and beard were as white as snow. He was as much altered in character as in appearance, and his first care ever after was to discharge every duty with the utmost conscientiousness, and to use only his leisure moments to indulge in his favorite pastime, the chase.

Clemenskapelle
The Alraun

I t is a well-known tradition that when a man who is a thief by inheritance—that is to say whose father, grandfather and great-grandfather before him had all been thieves or whose mother committed a theft while pregnant—would one day find himself on the gallows. At the foot of the gallows, would spring up a plant of hideous form known as the Alraun, or Gallows Mannikin. It is an unsightly object to look at, with broad, dark green leaves a single sickly yellow flower. The plant has great powers and whosoever possesses it will never want for money.

It is a feat full of the greatest danger to obtain this plant. If not taken up from the root, clean out of the soil, it is altogether valueless, and he who makes the attempt wantonly forfeits his life. The moment the earth is struck with the sap the bitterest cries and shrieks burst forth from it, and while the roots are being laid bare demons are heard to howl in horrid concert. When the preparatory work is done, and when the hand of the daring man is laid on the stem to pluck forth his prize, then it is as if all the fiends of hell were let loose upon him, such shrieking, such howling, such clanging of chains and such crashing of thunder and such flashing of forked lightning assail him on every side. If his heart fail him for but one moment, his life is forfeited. Many a bold heart engaged in this trial has ceased to beat under the fatal tree; many a brave man's body has been found mangled and torn to pieces on that accursed spot.

There is happily, however, only one day in the month — the first Friday — on which this plant appears. On the night of that day only, may it be plucked from its hiding-place. The way it is done is this: whosoever seeks to win it fasts all day. At sundown, he sets forth on his fearful adventure, taking with him a coal-black hound, which has not a single fleck of white on its whole body, and which was compelled likewise to fast for four-and-twenty hours. At midnight, he takes his stand under the gallows, and there stuffs his ears with wool or wax, so that he may hear nothing. As the dread hour arrives, he stoops down and makes three crosses over the Alraun, and then commences to dig for the roots in a perfect circle around it. When he has laid it entirely bare, so that it only holds to the ground by the points of its roots, he calls the hound to him and ties the plant to its tail. He then shows the dog some meat which he flings a short distance from the spot. Ravenous with hunger, the hound springs after it, dragging the plant up by the roots, but before he can reach the tempting morsel he is struck dead as if by some invisible hand.

The adventurer, who all the while stood by the plant to aid in its uprooting should the strength of the animal prove insufficient, then rushes forward and, detaching it from the body of the dead hound, grasps it firmly in both hands. First washing it well in red wine, he then wraps it up carefully in a silken cloth, and then bears it homeward. The hound is buried in the spot whence the Alraun had been plucked.

On reaching home, the man deposits his treasure in a strong chest with three locks, and visits it only every first Friday of the month, or rather, after the new moon. On these occasions he again washes it with red wine, and enfolds it afresh in a clean silken cloth of white and red colors.

If he has any questions to ask, or any request to make, he then puts the one or proffers the other. If he wishes to know of things in the future, the Alraun will tell him true, but he will get only one answer in the moon, and nothing else will be done for him by the plant. If he desires to obtain some substantial favor, he has it performed for him on making his request, but then the Alraun will answer no inquiries as to the future until the next day of visitations shall arrive.

Whosoever has this wonder of the world in his possession can never take harm from his foes, and never sustain any loss. If he be poor, he at once becomes rich. If his marriage be unblessed by offspring, he at once has children. If a piece of gold be laid beside the Alraun at night, it is found to be doubled in the morning, and so on for any sum whatsoever, but never has it been known to be increased more than two pieces for each one.

On the demise of the owner, only a youngest son can inherit the Alraun. To inherit it effectually, he must place a loaf of white bread and a piece of money in the coffin of his father, to be buried along with his corpse. If he fails to do so, then is the possession, like many others of great name in the world, of no value to him. Should, however, the youngest son fail before his father, then the Alraun rightfully belongs to the eldest, but he must also place bread and money in the coffin of his brother, as well as in that of his father, to inherit it to any purpose.

Bingen, *Heath's Picturesque Annual (1833)*

Bingen
The Mice's Tower

In the year 914, when Hatto was bishop of Mainz, a long season of rain ruined the entire harvest. A terrible famine arose from which the poor people suffered sorely. As they were perishing with hunger, they finally applied to the bishop, whose granaries were filled to overflowing with the produce of former, more favorable, years.

But Hatto was cruel and hardhearted and utterly refused to listen to them. At last, they so wearied him by their constant begging that he finally asked them to assemble in an empty barn. "I'll meet you there and quiet all your demands," he vowed.

Almost beside themselves with joy at this promise, the people hastened to the appointed spot, gathering there in such numbers that the empty barn was soon quite full. Anxiously they watched for the bishop, whom they greeted with loud cries of joy as soon as he appeared. These acclamations, however, were soon changed into blood curdling cries of distress. The cruel prelate, after bidding his servants fasten doors and windows so that none could escape, set fire to the moldering building and burned them all, declaring, "You beggars are like mice, and should be treated as such."

When the wholesale massacre ended, the bishop returned home. He sat down before his lavishly spread table and ate with as healthy an appetite as usual. Guilt did not trouble him and he retired to an undisturbed rest.

When he entered the dining room on the morrow, however, he stood shock still in dismay. During the night mice had entered from Lord knew where and had gnawed his recently finished portrait out of the frame. The tattered remains lay in a pile on the floor. While he was standing over it, his heart filled with sudden nameless terror, a servant came rushing into the room. "Fly! Fly for your life! There is a whole army of hungry, fierce looking mice coming this way!"

Without waiting for his usual escort, the bishop flung himself upon his steed and rode rapidly away. From time to time, he nervously turned his head to mark the gradual approach of a dark line formed by thousands of mice, animated by the revengeful spirits of the poor he had so cruelly burned.

Faster and faster Hatto urged his panting steed, but in spite of all his efforts, he had scarcely dismounted, entered a small skiff and rowed out into the Rhine, ere an army of mice fell upon his horse and devoured it. The bishop, shuddering with fear, rowed with all his might to his tower in the middle of the Rhine, where he quickly locked himself in, fancying he had escaped from his hungry foes.

But the voracious mice, having disposed of his steed, now boldly swam across the river to the tower. They swarmed rapidly up its sides, seeking some crevice through which they could get at their foe. As they found none, they set their sharp teeth to work, and Hatto quailed with dread as he heard them gnawing busily on all sides. In a very few moments the mice had made a thousand holes through which they rushed upon their victim.

Ever since then, that building in the Rhine has been known as the Mice's Tower. Tradition relates that the bishop's soul sank down to the nethermost hell, where it is ever burning in a fire far hotter than that he kindled around the starving poor. At sunset, a peculiar red glow may be seen over the tower and this, the people declare, is only a faint reflection of that infernal furnace, sent to warn all mankind against cruelty to God's poor.

Daun
The Monkey Nurse

One of the Rheingrafs once lived in the pretty castle of Daun, of which nothing but ruins now remain. He assigned the sunniest room for the nursery of his little heir who, although motherless, was constantly watched and tended by a faithful old nurse. In the castle there was a monkey, which ranged about the place at will. Often it came into the nursery and gravely sat in a corner, watching the nurse handle the babe.

One day, after putting her little charge to sleep, the nurse sat down beside it and was soon lost in slumber herself. When she awoke and glanced at the cradle, she was terrified, for the babe was missing! The poor woman, conjecturing that he had been stolen by gypsies, and fearing her master's anger, ran and hid in the depths of the neighboring forest.

It was there that she heard a peculiar sound, and gazing cautiously through the bushes, saw the babe seated on the moss while the monkey amused him with red apples and gay flowers. The child must have crawled off unseen into the forest, and the monkey followed. The little creature imitated the nurse's gestures with the most absurd precision. In a few moments, however, the child began to cry, and the monkey taking it up gently, began to dandle it, and swinging gently backward and forward soon put it to sleep. Then he laid it down on the soft moss and, still imitating the old woman closely, clasped his hands in his lap and fell asleep. The nurse crept cautiously out of the thicket, recovered the babe, and hastened homeward. She found the whole castle in an uproar, for they had been missed. So caught, she was obliged to confess all that had occurred.

In gratitude for the recovery of his child, the Rheingraf placed a carving above the gateway representing a monkey amusing a babe with an apple, and ever since then the monkey has figured on the escutcheon of that noble family.

Rüdesheim
A Broken Vow

A fisherman once paused at Rüdesheim to pray at the shrine of St. Nicholas. For the first time in his life, he was about to encounter the dangers of the Binger Loch, a most treacherous stretch of the Rhine which his companions had described so vividly as to fill his simple heart with nameless fear. "Oh, good St. Nicholas," he prayed, "if you will only guide me safely over, I will give you a taper as tall and thick as the mast of my vessel."

Strengthened by this prayer he re-entered his vessel, pushed away from the shore, trimmed his sail, and was soon gliding over the dreaded waters. But the Binger Loch was as smooth as the most placid lake. The boatman looked around him in wonder and then exclaimed, "Fool that I was to believe my companions' tales of the Binger Loch, and to stop and pray at St. Nicholas' shrine! I won't give him the big taper I promised, but a two-penny dip!"

Scarcely had these words left his lips, however, than the smooth waters became rough, and the gentle breeze changed into a hurricane. The little bark, caught in the terrible eddy, was whirled around and suddenly sucked down into the vortex with the boatman and all his crew.

Since then, vows made at St. Nicholas' shrine have been scrupulously paid, for all the river boatmen are afraid of suffering the fate of their sacrilegious companion.

Johannisberg
The Corkscrews

The beautiful castle of Johannisberg stands in the midst of the most productive vineyards along the Rhine. This castle is built on the site of an old monastery dedicated to St. John, and if the legend is true, it is very evident that those ancient monks knew how to appreciate the product of their own vines.

One day the prior invited all the brethren to accompany him on an inspection tour of the monastery vineyards. This invitation was accepted with evident pleasure by all. After they had walked a long while along the sunny slopes between the loaded vine, they reached a shady spot. The prior proposed that they all sit down, rest and refresh themselves morally and physically by reading the afternoon prayers and drinking a few bottles of delicious old wine, which they had brought with them. Again the monks joyfully acquiesced, but when the prior asked for a breviary, they all hung their heads and confessed that they had forgotten to bring them along. The jovial prior good naturedly remarked that since there was no prayerbook handy, they would forego spiritual refreshment and proceed with the physical. He took up one of the bottles and vainly attempted to remove the cork with his fingers. Turning to the assembled brothers, he asked whether any had brought a corkscrew.

Simultaneously the monks thrust their hands into their pockets and each eagerly produced a corkscrew. The prelate accepted one of them, uncorked one of the bottles, and as he raised the goblet of sparkling wine to his thirsty lips, he dryly remarked with a twinkle in his eye, "Not a single breviary, but plenty of corkscrews. Is that a proof of your zeal in serving the Lord?"

The monks hung their heads and quaffed the wine in silence, but temporary embarrassment soon passed, and erelong they were drinking merrily, and pledging their favorite saint—John.

Oestrich
The Revengeful Ghost

Near the village of Oestrich once rose the renowned convent of Gottesthal, where many a holy nun spent her life in penance and prayer. The town's legends relate that a neighboring knight, falling desperately in love with one of the convent inmates, prevailed upon her to forget her vows and meet him every evening in the chapel. There he promised ever to be faithful to her, even if they could never be married, owing to her vows.

The knight was a rover, however, and soon forgot the pretty nun, who pined and grew pale when she heard he was courting another. The rumor of these doings was soon confirmed, and the perjured nun, mad with jealously and despair, hired an assassin to slay the lover who had deceived and deserted her.

The knight's remains were duly interred in the same chapel where he had come so often to woo the little nun. That night, when the midnight hour struck, the door opened, a closely veiled figure stole to his tomb, opened it, and with muttered curses and shrieks of rage tore his base heart out of his body and trampled it wildly under foot.

The veiled figure was the nun, driven insane by remorse and grief, and many years after that her ghost returned at midnight, dragged the knight from his tomb, tore out his heart and trampled it, while her shrieks echoed through the ruins. Now no trace of convent or chapel remains, and the ghost is no longer seen, but her despairing cries of rage can still be heard from time to time. The poor beleaguered soul will never cease to hate her faithless lover.

Elfeld
The Rope of Hair

A reckless knight called Ferdinand once dwelt at Elfeld on the Rhine. When he had duly squandered all his patrimony and found himself too poor to purchase an outfit to attend a tournament given in honor of the queen, he vowed life was no longer worth living, and rushed out of the castle to commit suicide. He was about to cast himself headlong into the river, when Satan suddenly appeared before him and offered him a heavy purse of gold in exchange for a single hair. The knight accepted; the exchange was made, and the devil vanished, promising to return whenever the knight summoned him. "I will furnish you with an equal sum of pure gold for every hair which you allow to be plucked from your head."

The sum thus furnished by Satan was quite sufficient for the knight's present needs, so he agreed. Sooner than expected he exhausted his fortune and called out for Satan. In exchange for another hair, he received another bag full of gold. Little by little, the knight grew more reckless, the devil's visits more frequent, and the knight's head so bald that it attracted playful attention from his friends.

Finally, after a long, dissipated life, the knight fell dangerously ill. Unwilling to bear the pain he would fain have committed suicide, but had no strength left to go in search of his sword to plunge into his breast. While he was bemoaning his helplessness and loudly calling for someone to end his wretched existence, the devil appeared and gave him a rope fashioned entirely out of the hair plucked from his head. "I have fashioned you a noose, good sir knight, that you might hang yourself."

On the morrow, the doctors found him dead with a hair noose drawn tightly around his neck and an expression of fear upon his dead face. The devil had carried away his soul.

Mainz
The Street Sweeper

Once, when the French army occupied Mainz and the country was groaning under the harsh rule of the invader, the young ladies of the city—spurred on by the beautiful young Countess of Stein—solemnly vowed that they would neither marry nor listen to a word of love from any man until their country was entirely free.

The Frenchmen, hearing of this league and seeing that it raised the ardor of their foes to attack them with renewed courage, angrily resolved to make an example of the young Countess of Stein. They dragged her, a prisoner, into the city, publicly thrust a broom in her hand, and bade her sweep the principal street.

Instead of bursting into tears as they expected, the noble girl grasped her broom firmly, and gazing upward, prayed aloud, "God of my fatherland, bless my sweeping, and as I sweep the highway, grant that the enemy may be swept from our land."

She set vigorously to work, sweeping the road very clean. Although the Frenchmen stood on either side of the street, twisting their mustaches until they stood straight out like needles, waiting to hear the people jeer, they saw nothing but uncovered heads and heard nothing but low and fervent praises of, "God bless the sweeping!" Fired by the courage of the young countess, the men now fought with a will and succeeded at last in sweeping the enemy completely out of their land.

Falkenstein
The Gnomes' Road

K uno von Sayn, of the noble family whose ruined castle still rises on one of the hills along the Rhine, once fell in love with the daughter of the surly Lord of Falkenstein. Having won her consent, he set out to present himself before her father to ask her hand in marriage.

He climbed the hill to the castle of Falkenstein, which was perched on the heights above one of the tributaries of the Main River. The youth made his proposal and awaited his answer. After many tense moments, Lord Falkenstein said, "I will honor your suit, but on one condition."

"Anything, my Lord!" the impetuous lover vowed, not even waiting to inquire what the condition might be. Imagine his chagrin and dismay when Lord Falkenstein told him, "You may wed my daughter, but only if you build a road from this castle to the next valley, up and over the jagged rocks. By sunrise tomorrow I hope to be able to ride my war steed along it."

"But my Lord..." the young man protested.

"Enough! You have agreed to my terms and I have given you a task. You may even seek help if you wish; such is my generosity. Now go!"

Sadly, Kuno von Sayn scrambled down the rocks again without having been able to catch even a glimpse of the fair Irmengarde, his beloved. He sat down upon a rock in the valley and berated himself for his stupidity. Even with a score of workmen and many months of hard labor, he would scarcely accomplish the task!

Suddenly, however, he was pulled from his self-pity by the sound of a little voice calling him by name. He looked up and beheld the king of the gnomes, who jovially said, "No need for despair, Kuno. My subjects and I would gladly aid such a deserv-

Riding up the Falkenstein, *by Moritz von Schwind (1843-44)*

ing knight. Now go back to the inn and get a good evening's rest. When you come back at sunrise the road will be finished." Then the king of the gnomes waved his hand and caused a mist to rise and shroud valley and hill with its dense vapor.

Thousands of dwarf-like creatures now crept out of the ground on all sides and began using axes, hammers and spades with great good will. All night long Kuno von Sayn sat by his window, too nervous to sleep, and heard the crashing of great forest trees, the breaking of stone and occasionally a loud rumble like thunder. At dawn he emerged from his bedroom and was greeted by the innkeeper.

"Judging by the noise which kept us all awake, a terrible storm must have raged over the valley," the innkeeper said. Kuno did not pause to listen to the man's tales, but loudly called for his horse and rode rapidly away to the foot of the peak upon which rose the castle of Falkenstein. True to his promise, the king of the gnomes had built a broad and convenient road, and Kuno galloped boldly up, exchanging radiant smiles with the kindly dwarfs who peered out at him from behind every rock and tree. As he thundered over the arched bridge they were just finishing, he gayly waved his hand to Irmengarde who, blushing and happy, stood up on the castle ramparts. Then the dwarfs unanimously raised a glad shout of triumph.

Lord Falkenstein, seeing his condition had duly been complied with, could no longer refuse his consent to his daughter's speedy marriage with Kuno von Sayn. The first sunbeams of the morning, falling upon the castle, illuminated the golden hair and blushing cheeks of the maid, who was joyfully clasped close to her lover's heart.

Frankfort
The Executioner

A grand masked ball was once given in the town hall of Frankfort on the Main, in honor of the king and queen who, also disguised, mingled with their guests. Her Majesty even accepted partners in the dance, and twice trod a measure with a tall, distinguished-looking man whose reserved but courtly manners greatly pleased her.

As none of her eager questions had elicited any answer which could enable her to discover who he might be, she resolved to watch him when he unmasked, and even gave the signal for it by removing her own disguise a whole hour earlier than usual. All the guests immediately imitated her with the exception of the stranger. Only when compelled to do so by the queen's explicit command did he tear the mask away from his face. Falling down upon his knees before her, he craved her pardon for having presumed to ask her to dance.

"I don't understand," said the queen, a frown creasing her brow. "Why should you presume to have offended me? Tell, me, what is your name?"

As she gazed down at the handsome face, waiting for an answer, a voice in the crowd shouted, "Is it not the executioner of Bergen?"

"How dare he insult us with his presence!" shouted another.

"Yes," replied the stranger sorrowfully, "I am the executioner of Bergen, and because I do the king's will I am shunned and scorned by all. All flee from me and loath me as if I were not of their own kind. The longing to once again mingle with my fellow creatures drove me to your party."

The king, hearing these words, was so indignant that he called for his guards. "Drag this man away for so insulting my queen by dancing with her. Behead him with his own axe!"

Before this order could be executed, however, the man cried out, "Even if I am slain the queen will none-the-less have danced with the vilest of the commoners. Anyone could taunt her with the fact, and even blood would never efface the stain."

With a groan the king acknowledged that this was true. "But," the executioner continued, "I am ready to defend her against any man. Make me a knight, and I will fight all injustice in her name!" The king agreed, and seizing his sword gave the executioner the title of knight and bade him rise, calling him the Knave of Bergen.

"Rise, my champion," said the queen kindly, and thus was the executioner saved from death and admitted among the nobility of the land.

The Drachenfels, *Heath's Picturesque Annual (1833)*

Auerbach
Doctor All-Wise

There was once a poor peasant named Crab who drove two oxen with a load of wood into the city, and there sold it to a doctor for two thalers. The doctor counted out the money to him as he sat at dinner; the peasant, seeing how well he fared, desperately wanted to be a doctor, too. He stood a little while in thought, and at last asked if he could not become a doctor.

"Oh, yes," said the doctor, "that may be easily managed. In the first place you must purchase an ABC book, taking care that it is one that has in the front of it a picture of a cock crowing. It will provide you with all the answers you need. Sell your cart and oxen and use the money to buy new clothes and all the other things you might need. Thirdly and lastly, paint a sign with the words 'Doctor All-Wise' and nail it up before the door of your house."

The peasant did exactly as he had been told. After he had doctored for a little while, it chanced that a certain nobleman was robbed of a large sum of money. Someone told him that there lived in a village hard by a Doctor All-Wise, who was sure to be able to tell him where his money had gone. The nobleman at once ordered his carriage to be made ready and rode into the city, and having come to the right house asked, "Are you Dr. All-Wise?"

"Oh yes," answered Crab. "I am Doctor All-Wise sure enough."

"Will you go with me, then?" asked the nobleman. "And get me back my money?"

"To be sure, I will," said the doctor, "but my wife Gretel must go with me."

The nobleman was pleased to hear this. He had them both get into the carriage with him and away they all rode together. When they arrived at the nobleman's house, dinner was already prepared, and he asked the doctor to sit down with him.

"My wife Gretel, too," said the doctor.

As soon as the first servant brought in the first dish, which was some great delicacy, the doctor nudged his wife and said, "Gretel, that is the first," meaning the dish. His wife was somewhat deaf and needed to read her husband's lips.

But the servant overhead the doctor's remark and thought he meant to say he was the first thief, which was actually the case, so he was sorely troubled and said to his comrades, "The doctor knows everything. Things will certainly fall out ill, for he said I was the first thief."

The second servant refused to believe they had been discovered, but at last he was obliged, for when he carried the second dish into the room, the doctor remarked to his wife, "Ah, that is the second."

The second servant was now as much frightened as the first, and was pleased to leave the dining chamber. The third servant fared no better, for the doctor said, "Gretel, there is the third."

Now the fourth carried in a dish which had a cover on it, and the nobleman desired the doctor to show his skill in guessing what was under the cover. The doctor looked at the dish, and then at the cover, and could not at all divine what they contained, nor how to get out of the scrape. At length he said, half to himself and half aloud. "Alas, poor Crab, you've been found out."

When the nobleman heard this he cried, "You have guessed it! We're having crab for dinner! Now I am sure you will know where my money is."

The servant was greatly troubled at this, and he motioned for the doctor to follow him out of the room. No sooner did he do so than the thieves who had stolen the gold stood before him. "We will give up the gold instantly, and give you a good sum to boot, provided you do not betray us. If you do, our necks will surely pay for it."

The doctor promised, and they conducted him to the place where the gold lay concealed. The doctor was well pleased to see it, and went back to the nobleman and said, "My Lord, I will now search in my book and discover where the money is."

Now a fifth servant had crept into an oven to hear what the doctor said, ready to kill him if he did not keep his promise. He watched as the doctor thumbed through the leaves of his ABC book, looking for the picture of the crowing cock. As he did not find it readily, the doctor muttered, "I know you are in here, and you must come out."

Then the man hiding in the great oven, thinking the doctor spoke to him, jumped out in great fright, saying, "The man knows everything!"

Doctor All-Wise showed the nobleman where the gold was hidden, but he said nothing as to who stole it, so he received a great reward from all parties, and became a very famous man.

Frankfort on the Main, *Heath's Picturesque Annual (1833)*

Heidelberg
The Wolf's Spring

When the old pagan gods and goddesses were still worshiped in the Rhine country, a priestess of Herthe took up her abode in an ancient oak grove. There she practiced her occult arts so successfully that the fame of her divinations spread far and wide, and men came from all parts of Europe to learn from her what the future had in store.

Frequently a warrior left her abode with a consuming fire kindled in his breast, which would rob him of sleep for many a long night. Yet none dared to declare his love to her. Lovely though Jette was, there was an air of mysticism about her which commanded awe and reverence, and forbade even the smallest familiarity.

One evening there came to the grove of Herthe a youth from a far distant land, seeking to know his destiny. All day he had journeyed without rest, and dusk had already fallen before he reached the sacred spot. Jette sat on the glimmering altar-steps, clad in a flowing white robe, while on the altar itself burned a faint and fitful flame. The tall, slender trees, showing fantastic and ghostly in the fading light, made a fitting background for the gleaming shrine. The elusive, unearthly beauty of the priestess was quite in keeping with the magic scene. Her mantle of austerity had fallen from her; she had forgotten that she was a prophetess. For the moment she was but a woman, full of grace and charm. The youth paused as though held by a spell.

"Fair Prophetess," he said in a low voice, fearing to break in rudely upon her meditations, "will you read me my fate?"

Jette, roused from her reverie, fixed her startled gaze on the handsome stranger. His dark, burning eyes met hers in deepest admiration. Something stirred in her heart at the ardent glance and the thrilling tones; her composure deserted her. "Youth," she faltered at length, "you come at a time when my prophetic skill has failed me. Before I tell you your fate I must offer sacrifice to Herthe. If you will come tomorrow at this hour I will tell you what the stars say concerning your destiny."

It was true that her skill had deserted her under the admiring scrutiny of the young warrior. Yet she delayed also because she wished to hear his voice again, to meet the ardent yet courteous glance of his dark eyes.

"I will return, oh Prophetess," said he, and with that he was gone.

Jette's peace of mind had gone too, it seemed, for she could think of naught but the handsome stranger. On the following evening, he returned, and again she delayed to give him the information he sought. He was no less rejoiced than was Jette at the prospect of another meeting.

On the third day the priestess greeted him with downcast eyes. "I cannot read your destiny," she said, "the stars do not speak plainly. Yet I think your star and mine are very close together." She faltered and paused.

"Do you love me, Jette?" cried the young man joyfully. "Will you be my wife?" The maiden's blushing cheeks and downcast glance were sufficient answer.

"And will you come to my tower?" pursued the youth eagerly.

Jette started back in a fright. "No, I cannot do that! A priestess of Herthe is doomed if she marries. If I wed you, we must meet in secret and at night."

"But I will take you to Valhalla, and Freya shall appease Herthe with her offerings," he smiled.

Jette shook her head. "No, it is impossible. The vengeance of Herthe is swift—and awful. I will show you a spring where we may meet, perhaps without her notice." She led him to a place where the stream branched off in five separate rivulets, and bade him meet her there on the following night at a certain hour. The lovers then parted, each full of impatience for the return of the hour of meeting.

Next evening, when the dusk had fallen on the sacred grove of Herthe, Jette made her way to the rendezvous. The appointed

Heidelberg, *Heath's Picturesque Annual (1833)*

time had not yet arrived, but scarcely had she reached the spot before she fancied she heard a step among the undergrowth, and turned with a glad smile, prepared to greet her lover. Imagine her dismay when instead of the youth a grisly wolf confronted her! Her shriek of terror was uttered in vain. A moment later the monster had sprung at her throat.

Her lover, hastening with eager steps toward the place of meeting, heard the agonized shriek and, recognizing the voice of Jette, broke into a run. He was too late! The monster wolf stood over the lifeless body of his beloved, and though, in his despairing fury, the youth slew the huge brute, the retribution of Herthe was complete.

Henceforth the scene of the tragedy was called the Wolf's Spring, and the legend is enshrined there to this day.

Heidelberg
Legends of the Castle

Frederick the Victorious, who once dwelt in the castle of Heidelberg, was attacked by the allied knights and bishops of the Rhine. Undaunted by the superior numbers of his foes, he made a bold sally with his men. They were all armed with sharp daggers instead of the usual weapons, and first attacked the horses instead of the riders. Thus brought to the ground, the knights, unable to move in their ponderous armor, were soon made prisoners and marched into Heidelberg Castle. To their surprise, Frederick invited them all to partake of a sumptuous banquet.

As he sat at the richly spread board with his enemies, Frederick served them bountifully. There was meat and wine in abundance, but the guests gazed at each other in puzzlement, for there was no bread. This strange omission on the bill of fare was not an oversight, however, for when one of the guests ventured to ask for a piece of bread, the elector, turning to the steward, bade him bring some. The man, who had received private instructions, respectfully informed his master that he was very sorry but that there was none.

"Go and bake some!" commanded Frederick.

"Master, I can't. We have no flour."

"Have some ground."

"Master, I can't. We have no grain."

"Have some thrashed."

"I cannot. The harvests have all been burned."

"Then, go and sow grain that we may soon have bread in plenty."

"Master, I cannot, for the enemy has also burned down all the peasants' barns and dwellings with the grain set aside for seed time."

Frederick then dryly remarked as he turned to his guests, "Gentlemen, you'll have to eat your meat without bread. Moreover, you must give me the necessary funds to rebuild the houses and barns that you have burned down, and to buy seed for sowing. Henceforth, I advise you to remember that it is not right to make war against the poor and defenseless, and to rob the peasant of his tools and seed, his only means of subsistence. If you do so, you will invariably find, as today, that you too must suffer some discomfort in return for all the harm you have done."

Speyer Cathedral

Speyer
The Two Bells

I n the city of Speyer, there once hung two bells which were
never rung by human hands, but were said to toll of their
own accord. One, made of pure silver, was called the Emperor's
Bell, for it softly tolled when an imperial soul was called away.
The other, made of iron, was the Sinner's Bell, and rang whenever a notoriously wicked person breathed his last.

On one occasion, a poor old man lay dying on the damp
straw in a hovel in Speyer, and as his spirit passed away, the
Emperor's Bell began to ring a mournful knell. The people all
rushed out in surprise, for Henry was perfectly well. They loudly
wondered how the generally discriminating bell could make
such a mistake when they heard that it was only a poor old beggar who had just died.

That self-same night, however, in spite of the sentinel watching the palace gate, the angel of death stole in and called the
emperor away. Henry V, who recognized no superior on earth
and followed only his own sweet will, was forced to obey the
summons. And, as his soul reluctantly went forth to meet his
maker, the Sinner's Bell began to toll. The people, turning over
sleepily in their beds, declared it was evident some very wicked
person had passed away.

When they discovered the true state of affairs on the morrow,
they crossed themselves in awe and whispered, "The last shall be
first and the first last." Then they added that the bells had
proved to all that a virtuous death amid poverty was more wor-
thy of honor than the death of an unrepentant sinner at court,
and that the souls of the good were imperial in God's sight.

Neueberstein
The Count's Leap

The castle of Neueberstein, which towers above the Murg, a tributary of the Rhine, was once held under siege by the Württembergers. There they solemnly vowed to remain until they had starved Count Wolf von Eberstein to death or until he surrendered.

Aware that nothing would induce the Württembergers to take back this vow, and anxious to save his garrison from a slow death by famine, the daring Lord of Eberstein mounted his favorite steed and galloped wildly along the ramparts, suddenly making a leap down into the swollen river below.

The enemy, who had viewed this rash leap, rushed to the steep banks of the river and saw master and steed rise safely, breast the tide, and vanish in the forest. The prisoner having flown, the Württembergers raised the siege. But when the account of this prowess reached the emperor, he was so excited that he pardoned the count and permitted him to return to his fortress. Today, tourists can still see the famous spot, known as "The Count's Leap," from which he sprang into the river.

The Leap

Mummelsee
The Water Sprites

The almost circular sheet of water known as the Mummelsee, surrounded by rocky, pine-covered slopes, is said to be haunted by a water god, called Mummel, and by his numerous daughters, the beautiful nymphs known as Mummelchen. No fish are found in these waters, which generally lie smooth and unruffled in their dark bed.

The legends relate that a desperate poacher once slew the gamekeeper of the neighboring forest, and flung the body into the Mummelsee, thinking it would keep the secret of his crime. Before he could escape up the hillside, the irascible water god, who would not even allow a pebble to be cast into his domain, rose up out of the waters, caught him by the ankles and drew him down to the bottom of the lake, where he was drowned in punishment for his crime.

The daughters of old Mummel are said to rise up out of the lake on moonlight nights to dance on the green sward, clad all in white with glistening pearls and diamonds in their long golden hair. During the daytime these maidens, in the form of water lilies, rock gently upon the smooth waters and, as they are weary with the night's exertions, they fall sound asleep soon after the rising of the sun. Their grim old father is said to keep close watch over them, and when the first glimmer of dawn appears, he slowly rises out of the flood, beckons sternly to his dancing daughters, and imperiously commands them to return to their native element, and resume the flower-like form, which serves to delude mortals and conceals their true nature.

Strassburg
The Hot Porridge

The little town of Zurich, in Switzerland, once sought the alliance of Strassburg, but the magistrates of the larger city, thinking so small an ally of no importance, rudely declared that Zurich was too far away to lend them any assistance in case of need. Bluntly did they refuse the honor.

When the councilors of Zurich read the Strassburgers' answer, they were very indignant indeed, and talked of challenging them. The youngest among them, however, declared he would make them eat their words, and pledged his honor to bring a different answer erelong.

The other councilors agreed to let him arrange the matter as he pleased, and leisurely returned to their dwellings, while this man went home in a great hurry, selected the biggest pot in his kitchen and calling his wife, bade her cook as much oatmeal as it would contain.

Wondering greatly at this command, the woman quickly bade her servants build a roaring fire. Then she set to stirring and cooking the oatmeal. Meanwhile her husband rushed down to the quay, prepared his swiftest vessel, collected a number of the best oarsmen, and when all was ready, bade two of them accompany him home. He sprang breathless into the kitchen, and learned that the oatmeal was ready. "Quick, lift the pot from the fire!" he called to his men. "And carry it down to the boat!"

He followed them quickly, saw it placed in the stern, and turning to his men, exclaimed, "Now lads, row with all your might, for we are bound to prove to those stupid old Strassburgers that we are near enough to serve them a hot supper in case of need."

Inspired by these words the youths bent to the oars, and the vessel shot down the Limmat, Aar, and Rhine, leaving town, village, and farm in its wake, and only stopping when it reached the quay at Strassburg. The councilor sprang ashore, bade the two men follow with the huge pot, and striding into the council hall, had it set before the assembled magistrates. Breathless, he exclaimed, "Gentleman, Zurich sends a warm answer to your cold refusal."

With gaping mouths the Strassburgers gazed at the still steaming pot, and when the young Zuricher explained how it got there, they were so amused by the wit and promptitude which their would-be allies had displayed, that they unanimously voted for the alliance. It was duly signed and sealed ere they called for spoons. Laughing heartily, they ate every bit of the oatmeal, which was declared excellent, and proved hot enough to burn more than one councilor's mouth.

Ever since then, this huge iron pot, which is known as the pot of alliance, has been carefully preserved in the town hall of Strassburg, where it can still be seen.

A Giantess' Playthings, Rheinsagen *by Karl d'Efter*

Haslach
A Giantess' Playthings

In mythical ages there dwelt at Nideck, in Alsace, a mighty and gigantic race. The daughter of the Nideck giant, a damsel of colossal size, once started out for a walk. As her mode of locomotion consisted in clearing with a bound all intervening valleys, she soon arrived at Haslach, where for the first time in her life, she suddenly beheld a peasant plowing his field.

Delighted with the marvelous activity of these, to her, wonderful and tiny beings, she clasped her hands in rapture, then snatched up peasant, plow and team, and bundling them into her apron, ran home as fast as her legs could carry her.

"Father, see the pretty playthings I found yonder in the valley," she cried, opening her apron to let him see the new-found treasure.

"My daughter," said the giant gravely, "these are no playthings, but living creatures as well as we. Carry them quickly back to the place where you found them, and henceforth forbear to lay a finger upon them, for those tiny creatures are destined to be our supplanters."

Sorrowfully the giant maiden carried peasant, plow, and team back to the field, set them down in the unfinished furrow, and returned home, mourning the loss of the cunning playthings which she had not been permitted to retain.

Basel
From Castle to Cot

Not far from Basel rose the castle of Christopher of Ramstein who, having inherited it from spendthrift ancestors, soon found that he would be obliged to sell it in order to satisfy the claims of old creditors. Honorable in all things, Christopher sold all, reserving nothing for himself, and when the bargain was concluded, he divided the money among the assembled creditors, paying every debt in full.

Although not a penny was left when he had ended, and although he and his lovely young wife were homeless and destitute, Christopher of Ramstein stood proudly in their midst, thankful to know that no stain rested upon his name. The creditors, touched by his brave bearing, now crowded around him, offering him aid. He refused, saying he had hired a little dwelling; was about to till the soil for a rich farmer, and was sure that by the sweat of his brow he would be able to secure daily bread for himself and his wife, who had nobly encouraged him to do his duty.

The creditors insisted upon giving him something, however. He begged them to procure for his wife a silken dress, as he could not bear to see her attired in the rough garments they had assumed, for they had even sold their clothes to clear their debts. The silken garment was immediately ordered, and the Basel merchants furnished such good material that the dress lasted for many a year. Christopher, returning home from his work in the fields, had the satisfaction of seeing his lovely wife, clad as richly as of old, standing in the doorway of their humble cottage to welcome him home with the lovely kiss which made him forget toil and privation. Their mutual love enabled them to remain happy, though poor, as long as they lived.

Augst
The Snake Lady

At a short distance from Basel is the picturesque little town of Augst, and near here, according to the legend, is a hollow mountain in which a mysterious creature has taken up her abode. This creature, half woman and half snake, is detained there by a horrible spell, from which she can be released only if a pure youth voluntarily kisses her thrice. As the legend declares, she will reward her deliverer by giving him a great treasure, which she is guarding with the help of two baying hell hounds.

A handsome young man of Augst, named Leonard, was desirous to see her. He armed himself with a taper, which had been duly blessed by the priest, and venturing alone into the legendary valley, soon discovered an iron door in the mountainside. He quickly passed through it, along a corridor, and came at last to a beautiful cave, where he saw a lovely woman beckoning to him to draw near.

Beside her was a great chest, on either side of which sat two fierce hounds whose wild barking the lady stilled with a gentle wave of her hand. Then, taking a key from the bunch at her belt, she unlocked the chest, and the dazzled youth saw gold, silver, and precious stones in untold profusion.

"All these treasures will be yours, good youth, if you will only thrice kiss my lips," replied the lady, advancing toward him. Then Leonard noticed, for the first time, that although the upper part of her body was lovely indeed, the lower part was formed of the repulsive coils of a snake. After a moment's hesitation, however, he drew near and twice kissed the snake lady's lips, but, frightened by the swishing of her tail, he fled ere the last kiss had been given. In his terror he rushed out of the cave and into the town, where some youths, under pretext of helping him recover his senses, made him drunk, while extracting the particulars of his tale.

On the morrow, sober once more and longing to release the lady from the loathsome spell which bound her and to secure his reward, Leonard again set out. As he was no longer perfectly pure, however, he could not find the entrance to the cave. Since then many a youth has tried to find it and win the treasure, but as these young men had at some time in their life lied or stolen, drunk or sworn, they were not allowed to find the mysterious door, and the snake lady is still waiting for her deliverer.

Basel in the 17th Century

Pfafers
The Stolen Sacrament

The Devil once took up his abode in the narrow ravine whence the hot springs of Pfafers rise, and lying in wait there, soon saw Anna Vogtli pass by. He knew that she was a witch, and that she delighted in seeking herbs at midnight on the mountain side, so he promised her all manner of luck in her search if she would only steal into the neighboring church and throw away the holy wafer resting on the altar.

The girl, who had long ago given up going to mass and who had already sold her soul to Satan, immediately obeyed. But, no sooner had she laid her hand upon the sacred host than the ground shook; the lightning played; the thunder rolled, and the mountain echoes began to awaken. Terrified at the sudden commotion, Anna Vogtli threw away the wafer, which fell on a thorn bush. There sprang a silvery rose, which curled its petals all around the host to protect it from all harm.

Some sheep passing by there reverently bent the knee, and a wolf, springing out of the thicket to devour them, lay down like a lamb among them. The people, attracted by these miracles, plucked the silvery rose and laid it upon the altar of the church of Ettes Wyl, where it can still be seen, and is said to have very blessed and miraculous properties.

Farewell to the Rhine

Adieu to thee, fair Rhine! How long delighted
The stranger fain would linger on his way!
Thine is a scene alike where souls united,
Or lonely contemplation thus might stray,
And could the ceaseless vultures cease to prey
On self-condemning bosoms, it were here
Where nature, nor too somber, nor too gay,
Wild, but not rude, awful, yet not austere,
Is to the mellow earth as autumn to the year.

Adieu to thee again! A vain adieu!
There can be no farewell to scenes like thine,
The mind is colored by thy every hue;
And, if reluctantly the eyes resign
Their cherished gaze upon thee, lovely Rhine!
'Tis with the thankful glance of parting praise.
More mighty spots may rise—more glaring shine,
But none unite in one attaching maze.
The brilliant, fair, and soft—the glory of old days.

The negligently grand, the fruitful bloom
Of coming ripeness, the white city's sheen,
The rolling stream, the precipice's gloom,
The forest's growth, and Gothic walls between,
The wild rocks, shaped as they had turrets been,
In mockery of man's art; and there withal
A race of faces, happy as the scene
Whose fertile bounties here extend to all,
Still springing o'er thy banks, though empires near thee fall.

— Lord Byron

From Basel to
Ludwigshafen — Mannheim

Consulted Sources and Further Readings

The editor would like to acknowledge that the tales in this collection come from the following 19th Century sources.

The Rhine, Legends Traditions and History from Cologne to Mainz
Joseph Snowe
©1839, F.C. Westley, London.

Legends of the Rhine
A.H. Bernard
©1871, J. Halenza Publishing, Mayence

Nymphs, Nixies, Naiads: Legends of the Rhine
Mary Anna Evans
©1895, G.P. Putnam's Sons, New York

Legends of the Rhine
Helene Adeline Guerber
©1895, A.S. Barnes, New York

Legends of the Rhine from Basel to Rotterdam
David Kapp
©1867, J. Halenza Publishing, Mayence

Hero Tales and Legends of the Rhine
Lewis Spence
©1915, Frederick Stokes, New York

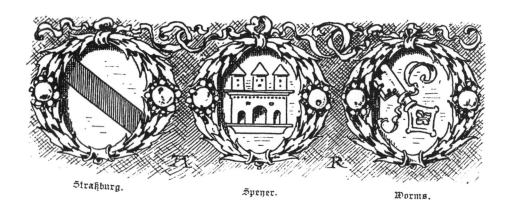

Straßburg.   Speyer.   Worms.

Basel

Säckingen

Rheinfelden

Laufenburg

Schaffhausen

Eglisau

Rheinau

Stein

Bodensee

Konstanz

Lindau

Bregenz

Aare

Zürich

Zürich-See

Zuger-See

Walen-See

Vaduz

Luzern

Vierwaldstätter-See

Ragaz

Vorderrhein

Hinterrhein

Tinzen

ST·GOTTHARD·P.

SPLÜGEN·P.

VOM
QUELLGEBIET
BIS
BASEL